DEADLINE DAY

DEADLINE DAY

The Inside Story of Football's Transfer Market

Jim White and Kaveh Solhekol

CONSTABLE

CONSTABLE

First published in Great Britain in 2023 by Constable

1 3 5 7 9 10 8 6 4 2

Copyright © Jim White and Kaveh Solhekol, 2023

The moral right of the authors have been asserted.

A CIP catalogue record for this book
is available from the British Library.

ISBN: 978-1-40871-818-6 (hardback)
ISBN: 978-1-40871-819-3 (trade paperback)

Typeset in Bembo by Hewer Text UK Ltd, Edinburgh
Printed and bound in Great Britain by Clays Ltd, Elcograf, S.p.A.

Papers used by Constable are from well-managed forests and other responsible sources.

Constable
An imprint of
Little, Brown Book Group
Carmelite House
50 Victoria Embankment
London EC4Y 0DZ

An Hachette UK Company

www.hachette.co.uk

www.littlebrown.co.uk

Contents

Chapter 1

Start Me Up

If you were buying or selling a house would you want all the twists and turns of the process covered by the media for months and months? Would you want the details of every offer on the back pages of the papers? Would you want people you had never met arguing on TV, radio and social media about how much your house is worth and whether it is a good investment?

Buying and selling a house is a stressful experience. Now imagine what it's like buying and selling a living and breathing human being. A human being who is so good at his job that lots of other people are fighting to pay millions and millions of pounds for him so he can work for them.

And unlike a house, this human being has feelings and he wants to have a say in who is going to buy him. His agent wants a say as well and so do his representatives and his advisers and his lawyers and his accountants – and don't forget his family.

Now, a house is a pretty solid investment and, all being well, it will be worth more than you paid for it when the time comes for you to move. There's also no chance of it collapsing in a heap, forcing you to buy another house to take its place while the house you spent a fortune on goes to Dubai to get better.

The human being you buy is going to have to be paid and you will have to indulge his every whim. And he may turn out to be not very good at his job. He may not settle in the area, his wife might not like the weather, his kids might not like the food and he might not like getting kicked by other human beings every weekend.

On top of all this, you are not buying this human being to keep. Despite the fact that you have paid millions of pounds for him and the same again in wages, he will be free to leave for absolutely nothing in about four years.

And don't forget, you won't be buying or selling just one human being. Every January and for three months in the summer you will be buying and selling lots of them. And the only thing that is guaranteed is that at least half of them will turn out to be a total waste of money.

Welcome to the wonderful world of transfers. They have been a big part of my life for more than twenty years and most of the time I absolutely love them. Some people hate transfers and some people love them, but deep down I know the people who hate transfers secretly love them too.

Don't get me wrong, I can see why in this day and age, with all the problems in the world, people think spending tens of millions of pounds on young men who do little more than kick a ball around is immoral. I get that. I understand why some fans think football is in danger of losing touch with reality, why it is now more business than sport. That is nothing new though. Football has been changing and evolving since the day it was invented.

I fell in love with football long before the days of transfer windows and £100 million deals and VAR and WAGs. I fell in love with the glory game, I looked up to the players, I idolised them and I felt an enormous thrill standing on the terraces with my father watching my heroes play for pride and their fans and the badges on their shirts.

The world moves on and everything changes and football is no different. What am I supposed to do? Give up on football because it has changed and moan and groan about what has happened to the game I fell in love with all those years ago? That's not in my nature. I still love football and I am naturally a very enthusiastic person.

Sure, there are lots of things I would change about the modern game if I could, but changing football is not my job. I don't own a club, I don't work at UEFA or FIFA, I am just a journalist who works hard and loves his job.

What gets me out of bed every morning is that inner drive to find things out and tell my viewers and listeners what is going on in the world of football. I love my job because I love football and I love journalism. There is no way you could do this job if you didn't love the game.

I understand the criticism, I understand the people who have fallen out of love with the game, the people who think it is all about money now. I understand the people who are irritated and bored by never-ending transfer sagas which dominate the headlines every summer. I can see why people think the sums being spent on transfers and the wages being paid are absurd. Believe me, I get all that. But at the same time, why should I be ashamed of what I do? Football, as someone once said, really is the most important of the unimportant things in life. It is for me and for millions of others as well.

I first got involved in transfers back in the eighties, when I was a young reporter at Scottish Television (STV). In those days there were no transfer windows and, for a period of time, Glasgow was the place to be. After the Heysel Stadium disaster in 1985, English clubs were banned from European competition. Rangers, under new player-manager Graeme Souness, embarked on a strategy of signing players from England. Playing at a magnificent stadium like Ibrox had always been a big draw but Rangers could also now offer English players the opportunity of playing in European competition. The club spent big money on players like Terry Butcher, Chris Woods, Mark Hateley and Trevor Steven.

I made sure I got to know as many players, managers and agents as I could so I could stay across all the comings and goings. That's when I first got to know Ally McCoist, who seemed to know everything about everybody, and an agent called Bill McMurdo, who looked after players like George Best and Mo Johnston. There were no mobile phones in those days so if I wanted to get in touch with someone like Bill I had to try my luck by calling him at home or at his office.

Modern technology has made all our lives a lot easier and more convenient but I sometimes still miss the thrill of the old days. In August 1991, I got wind of the fact that Trevor Steven could be moving from Rangers to Marseille in a £5.5 million deal. That was a seriously big transfer in those days so there was only one thing to do – get in my car and find him.

I made a few calls and managed to get a rough idea of where he lived in Edinburgh. I didn't have the exact address but that wasn't going to stop me. An hour later, I was in the beautiful suburb of Cramond with a cameraman in tow asking anyone who would stop to talk to me if they knew where Trevor Steven lived. Luckily enough, one of his neighbours pointed me in the right direction and a few minutes later I found Trevor in his garden.

'Trevor, it's Jim White from STV. Do you mind if I grab a quick word?'

Not for the first – or last – time in my career perseverance paid off and Trevor, after getting over the shock of finding me in his garden, gave me a few minutes of his time for an exclusive interview. It is more than thirty years ago now, but if Trevor's neighbour is reading this – thank you very much, sir. I still owe you a drink!

The world has changed enormously since those days and so have transfers. The really big change happened in 2002, when transfer windows were introduced in the Premier League. A window meant a deadline and that meant drama and wonderful theatre.

One of the reasons I still get excited about transfers is I am a fan myself and, like all fans, I want my club to sign the best players and my rivals to miss out on their targets. I think hope is the essence of transfers. I don't want to get too deep, but people need to have dreams. It's human nature to want tomorrow to be better than today so no matter how terrible your team have been this season, there is always a chance it will change when the window opens and they bring in a few new faces.

Of course, I am old enough to remember when transfers used to happen out of the blue, before summer and winter windows and deadlines. For instance, Manchester United fans of a certain age almost certainly remember the mornings they woke up and read in the paper that their club had signed Eric Cantona or Andy Cole.

I have to go a bit further back and to Scotland for my first transfer memory. It was way back in 1968 when my father Robbie told me that Rangers had signed a prolific forward from Hibernian called Colin Stein. To this day, I remember how exciting it was that Rangers had signed a goal machine like Stein. He turned out to be a brilliant buy and he scored the opening goal in the Nou Camp in 1972 when Rangers won the European Cup Winners' Cup by beating Dynamo Moscow 3–2. It's good to know that Stein is still part of the club to this day, working in hospitality at Ibrox on match days.

I was just as excited about transfers in those days as I am now. I understand how people feel when they stop me in the street to ask me who their club are going to sign or whether a particular deal is going to go through. It is actually astonishing how much people seem to know, especially the younger fans, about players and deals all over the world. When I was at a Liverpool game in 2022, all anyone seemed to want to talk to me about was whether they were going to sign Aurélien Tchouaméni. I had heard about the Monaco midfielder and I knew he was a hot property, but these kids seemed to know everything there was to know about him.

Unfortunately for them, Liverpool missed out on Tchouaméni because he moved to Real Madrid that summer in an £85 million deal. The kids knew what they were talking about, though, because Tchouaméni looked like a real player when I saw him score the opening goal in France's 2–1 win against England in the World Cup quarter-final in Qatar in December 2022.

Speaking to fans who stop me on the street or at games is a big part of my job and it is something I enjoy the vast majority of the time. I am not kidding when I say that, on some deadline days, I get stopped twenty or thirty times. It's no hardship for me to find time for people and engage with them, no matter who they are or who they support.

I can count on the fingers of one hand the times anyone has stopped me to say anything negative about transfers or deadline days. I think even the people who don't like transfers realise that a lot of it is just harmless fun. Not everyone likes everything. I understand transfers are not for everyone. It's a matter of taste and it's a matter of choice. If people don't like me or what I do, that's not a problem as far as I am concerned, they don't have to watch me or listen to me.

I find it funny how often people who stop me out and about ask me if I am really like this in real life. I'm not sure I know the answer to that question but I tell them that, unfortunately, I think I am. I have always been naturally enthusiastic and exuberant. We all only have a limited amount of time on this planet so what's the point of living your life with a glum face? You have to go for it, make the best of every situation, try and enjoy life as much as possible.

Believe me, I know that's not always feasible – but that's what I try to do. It sounds like a very simple philosophy but it seems to work for me. I know I'm not going to be doing this job for ever so I may as well try and enjoy myself while I can. Whether the audience enjoys it as much as I do is not for me to say.

The number one question I get asked on the street is where a certain player is going to go. Every year there are names which seem to be on everyone's lips. In 2022, it was Erling Haaland and more recently it has been Kylian Mbappé and Harry Kane. Haaland scored a lot of goals in Norway but it was in 2019, when he moved to Austrian club Red Bull Salzburg, that everyone started talking about him. It was well known in football circles that he would be leaving Austria in January 2020 and I really got down to work reporting on him when he started being linked with clubs in England.

Part of my job is to get to know people around up-and-coming players so I can get information about them as their career progresses. It took some effort and time, but I was able to make contact with people close to Haaland in 2019 and, over the years, I have had some pretty good information about his transfers.

In 2020, Haaland turned down the opportunity to move to clubs like Manchester United and Juventus and signed for Borussia Dortmund instead in a €20 million deal. I think United missed out on him then because they would not agree to have a release clause in his contract, whereas Dortmund thought it was worth taking the risk of being used as a stepping stone. That's because Haaland was the type of striker who would guarantee goals and, even with a release clause, you would make a big profit when you had to sell. In April 2022 Borussia Dortmund's chief executive Hans-Joachim Watzke was asked about the deal by German broadcaster Radio 91.2: 'We gave Erling Haaland a release clause . . . otherwise he would have gone to Manchester United.'

Sure enough, two years and more than fifty goals later, everyone was talking about Haaland's next move before the transfer window opened in the summer of 2022. All the biggest clubs in Europe wanted him, especially because his release clause was only £51 million. Real Madrid, Barcelona, Paris Saint-Germain, Manchester United, Liverpool and Chelsea were all after him but I had known for a long time that he would be signing for Manchester City.

How did I know? I had been told by people close to the player, but it was not the kind of information that I could shout from the rooftops. I had been told, in confidence, that he was heading to City, and I had to be discreet about how I let that information get out. This was not something that could be reported as breaking news, it was more a case of me stating, as forcefully as I could, that he would be heading to City whenever his name was being discussed on my radio show.

That is something that people looking in from the outside may not always appreciate about what transfer reporters can and can't say. A fair amount of the time, the information you are getting is 'for background only' and that means you cannot give away where the information is coming from and you cannot make a big headline out of it. It can be frustrating at times – especially when people are accusing you of making things up or not knowing what you are talking about – but we just have to grin and bear it and keep trusting and respecting our sources. I am glad to say Haaland has been an absolutely fantastic signing for City and he has been worth every penny they paid to bring him to the Premier League. I think it's fair to say his move to City already deserves to be regarded as one of the best transfers of all time. In his first season he scored fifty-two times and City won the Treble. He is going to have a long career at City, but if he does decide to move some day in the faraway future, say to Saudi Arabia or Real Madrid, I am confident I will be able to get the inside track on what is happening. That's assuming of course that someone still thinks it's worth paying me to do this job I love so much.

As for Haaland, you can only imagine what people at Manchester United think about all the goals he is scoring and the trophies he is lifting at City. Not only did United miss out on him when he moved from Salzburg to Dortmund in 2020, and again in 2022 when he moved from Dortmund to City, but they could have signed him for a bargain £4 million in the summer of 2018 when he was eighteen and playing in Norway for Molde.

At the time, he was being managed by the former Manchester United striker and future United manager Ole Gunnar Solskjær, who was so impressed with the way Haaland was developing he called his old club to tell them they should sign him. 'I called United and told them that I'd got this striker but they didn't listen,' Solskjær said, speaking at a dinner in Manchester in May 2023. 'I asked for £4 million for Haaland but they didn't sign him.'

That was one that got away, on more than one occasion, for United and there are a few that get away for journalists as well. Something else which people might not know about this job is that journalists who cover transfers really are aware of the fact that a lot of these deals are just not going to work out. Most deals look good on paper, but I would estimate that at least 50 per cent of them turn out to be what you would politely call a waste of money. I know we sometimes get a reputation for hyping up transfers but that is really not the case. In the back of my mind I am always aware, to varying degrees, that a deal I'm reporting on may not work out in the long run, but I still have to be enthusiastic about the way I cover the story, otherwise my viewers and listeners would fall asleep.

I am not a salesman so it's right to be sceptical when I have doubts about a deal, but at the same time I have to convey some of the drama of the occasion, the theatre of the deal. If you don't have that energy and drive about you then you are going to find it very difficult to find and keep an audience in this business.

One thing it's important to keep in mind is that we should not treat players as if they are pieces of meat being bought and sold. They are human beings with feelings so I find it very uncomfortable when they are being talked about as if they are just commodities to trade. I try and stay away from criticising players personally if a move has not worked out. There can be thousands of different reasons why a transfer fails.

As a journalist, it is always better to give people the benefit of the doubt and say the move just hasn't worked out rather than get stuck into the player and say, for example, that he is not good enough or he has a bad attitude. We don't know what goes on behind closed doors and I prefer to leave the opinions and the analysis to the experts – former players and managers – although it seems as if social media has given everyone a platform to grandstand about topics they often know very little about.

Of course, not all moves turn out as well as Haaland's from Dortmund to City. When they go wrong, it hurts club owners – the people who sign the cheques – even more than it hurts the fans. Do I feel sorry for them when things go wrong? You must be joking. I doubt they feel sorry for me when I make a mistake at work so why should I feel sorry for them?

Joking aside, though, I have got to know many owners over the years and I have to say the vast majority of them have their club's best interests at heart. There are a few bad apples and rogues and I do my best to hold them to account if I get to interview them but, believe me, more often than not, they are not very keen to speak to me, or any other journalists, in public.

When it comes to transfers, some owners love them and some owners hate them. The ones who love transfers love the thrill of the chase, the intrigue and the plotting, the negotiations and secret meetings and the endless messages, emails and phone calls. These men have often made fortunes in business so you would think they would be good at doing deals, but the transfer market has often flummoxed and bamboozled businessmen who have had no problems making millions and millions of pounds in other industries.

There are also some owners who are very wary of getting involved in transfers at all. Some of them think the whole thing is a circus and, no matter who they buy or sell, they are going to get ripped off by agents and intermediaries. I think a lot of them are worried about losing big money in deals and they see warning signs which are not always obvious to people looking in from the outside. It wouldn't surprise me if a lot of owners didn't secretly want to go back to the old days when players were basically tied to their clubs for the whole of their professional careers and there was a maximum wage they could be paid.

One player who reminds me of the old days because of the way he plays and the way he carries himself is Jack Grealish. Even his name sounds like a throwback to the black-and-white era. I have known Grealish since he was a youngster at Aston Villa and I got to meet him and his father, Kevin, on a visit to Villa Park when he was starting to make a real name for himself after breaking into the first team in 2015.

Grealish is a real personality with a cheeky chappy side to his character and he is a fabulous player to watch. There had been lots of interest in him over the years and both Manchester United and Tottenham Hotspur had been very keen on signing him. It was in the summer of 2020 that things really started to hot up though. Grealish had signed a new long-term Villa contract amid talk of a move to Manchester United. His new deal had a £100 million release clause which it was presumed nobody was going to pay any time soon.

Now you should never presume anything in football: fast forward to August 2021 and Manchester City let Villa know that they were willing to trigger the release clause. Luckily, I had managed to report the deal was going to happen six weeks before it was announced because I have good relationships with several people who were involved in the negotiations. I did get some angry messages though, having a go at me for saying the deal was as good as done when nothing was official.

'What are you on about? Jack's still a Villa player. He's still a Villa player.'

He wasn't for much longer and that ended up being good news for everyone because the deal turned out to be one which eventually suited all parties. City got the player they wanted, Jack got the move he wanted, and Villa got a big fee. City and Jack also won the Treble in the summer of 2023 and Villa qualified for Europe for the first time in thirteen years.

If only everything in the world of transfers worked out so well.

Chapter 2

Man Found Dead in Cemetery

Looking back, I didn't set out to be on TV or radio. I didn't grow up wanting to be a performer, or wanting to be rich and famous. I wanted to be a journalist and very quickly I realised that to be a good journalist I had to get my own stories and interviews. I knew that if I did that consistently, I would have a good chance of succeeding in my chosen career.

The only way to get stories and interviews is to know people and get on with them. It sounds simple when you put it like that, but if it was that easy everyone would be doing it. I was lucky enough to grow up in an era where there were lots of real local newspapers and regional TV stations and that is where I learned on the job after I passed my exams to become a qualified journalist.

It seems like everyone wants to be on TV or radio these days, everybody wants to be famous. If that's all you want, then you should go on a reality TV show or become an influencer – whatever that is. If you want to become a broadcast journalist, the most important thing is to be a journalist first.

You can't break transfer stories if you are not a journalist, you can't break transfer stories if you just want to be famous. It takes years of hard work and dedication to put yourself in a position where people are going to trust and respect you enough to confide in you and give you the kind of information that is going to help you break a story.

If you are not a real journalist at heart, you are going to find it very hard to survive on a day as manic and busy as transfer deadline day, let alone on other days of the year. If you are presenting a live rolling news show, often with only a skeleton script to guide you, you have to be across all the big stories, you have to call and message your contacts during ad breaks and you have to constantly update stories in real time for your viewers and listeners.

The modern media is full of people talking about stories and giving everyone their opinion. That's not my job and I don't think that's why people watch or listen to me when I am on TV or radio. My job, as well as presenting and hosting shows, is to find out things my audience don't already know, things they are interested in, and tell them what I have found out immediately in a clear and informative way. That's what I have tried to do for my whole career. I am a journalist and a football fan at heart, I am interested in all the stories I cover, I want to find out what is going to happen next and I want to tell my audience first.

I am lucky to meet a lot of people who have watched me on TV or listened to me on the radio. Working in football means there is always a lot to talk about, but the one question hardly anyone, including my friends or family, ever asks me is, 'What is it actually like to present or report live on air?' I don't blame people for not asking because I am the same when I meet other journalists, broadcasters, footballers or managers. There is usually so much to talk about that you hardly have time to ask the obvious questions, such as, 'What does it feel like to play in or commentate on a World Cup final? How do you prepare for it? What does it feel like when it starts and when it ends?'

In my world, football is what everyone wants to talk about, but I do occasionally get asked about my job, especially by aspiring young journalists. You can tell the ones who are really switched on because of the questions they ask. As well as everything to do with the latest football story and the team they support they ask you questions such as, 'What is it really like to broadcast to an audience you can't see or hear? How do you do it? Is it all an act? Are you really like that in real life? Are you just reading out a script the whole time? What do you when things go wrong? Do you ever watch or listen to your own shows?'

I am not sure the impression people have of me is who I really am, although I'm afraid it might be pretty close. You can never totally be yourself on television or radio and to a certain extent you have to put on a bit of an act. No matter how you are feeling, you have to be a slightly louder and more positive version of yourself. You can't be just who you are when you are sitting at home on the sofa watching a game. You have to be real, authentic and true to yourself, and at the same time you have do everything you can to engage with people and be as informative and entertaining, when appropriate, as possible.

It's only natural that if you are on TV or radio there are going to be people out there who don't like you, even though they have never met you or spoken to you. That didn't feel like a big issue before the rapid growth of social media, but now everyone who is watching or listening can say exactly what they want about you in real time while you are doing your job. The negativity out there doesn't really bother me because I don't read it and the people writing it don't really know me. They know the me they see and hear doing my job, but they probably don't know the pressures and constraints I am working under and they won't know what I am like when I am not working and they don't know I have interests that have nothing to do with football or transfers. I'd like to think if people knew me they'd like me. I treat everyone the same. It doesn't matter to me whether you own a Premier League club or you are a builder who has stopped me for a chat in the street. I am going to treat you in exactly the same way because that is just the way I am.

By the way, despite what you may think if you spend any amount of time doom-scrolling on social media, people are very, very friendly when you meet them out and about. I cannot remember the last time I had a bad encounter with a member of the public. I spend a lot of time travelling on public transport and going to games and walking around

London, and people love to stop and talk about football. They love to talk about their teams, what is going right and what is going wrong, who they are going to buy and who they are going to sell. It's part of my job to talk and listen and engage. If you are not in tune with what real fans are thinking and feeling, you wouldn't be able to do my job properly at all.

When I was living and working in Glasgow I did get in a few unpleasant scrapes but nothing too serious. I am perceived as being a Rangers fan so the Old Firm rivalry meant I occasionally got grief from Celtic fans, and I still do sometimes. It bothered me in those days – especially when I had been drinking – and there were a few occasions when I answered back when perhaps it would have been better to ignore it all and move on.

More recently, I have had a few unpleasant moments and one that sticks in my mind is the European Championship game between England and Denmark at Wembley in the summer of 2021. I went to the game with a few colleagues from talkSPORT and I was abused for being Scottish outside and inside the ground. The worst part of it was when someone called me an effing Scottish so-and-so inside Wembley and threw a pint of beer in my face. I kept my cool and didn't rise to the bait even though it wasn't easy.

When I was growing up in Scotland, it was unthinkable that people would behave like that in public. My father Robbie took me to as many games as he could and it was always a real thrill to go and watch the great teams like Rangers and Celtic. I always wanted to be journalist and I learned my trade by studying for a pre-entry journalism diploma at Napier College in Edinburgh. That diploma is still available at colleges around the UK and in my opinion it is still the best qualification to get if you want to be a journalist. In Edinburgh, I learned the basics of journalism, media law and ethics and, of course, shorthand, which I use to this day, although I am not sure I could achieve 120 words a minute like I used to in my heyday.

I was talking to one of my colleagues the other day about journalism courses and he told me something that really stuck with me. When he was doing his diploma, his tutor told his whole class they were going to spend the afternoon pretending their classroom was a newspaper office. Everyone had to go out into the college, talk to other students and teachers and everyone else who worked there, find a story, come back to the office and write it up.

She told them to get their pen and pads and leave straight away because they only had ninety minutes to complete the task. The classroom emptied quickly and, after a few minutes, there was only the tutor and my future colleague left in the room. The tutor didn't look happy. 'What are you doing?' she said. 'Get out there and get me a story now!'

Quick as a flash he replied, 'I'm not going anywhere. This is a newspaper office and someone has to be here to answer the phone in case someone calls in with a story.'

I'm happy to report that my colleague ended up finishing top of his class and he's gone on to have a long and successful career in journalism. Pulling a stunt like he did at college would never have occurred to me. Under similar circumstances, I would have been straight out of the door interviewing a teacher or a dinner lady to try and get a story good enough to be the front page splash in our student newspaper.

But I must have done something right at college, because I passed my exams and I got jobs at real newspapers such as the *Hamilton Advertiser* and the *East Kilbride News*, where we once ran the headline, MAN FOUND DEAD IN CEMETERY.

I was a general news reporter so I covered whatever story I was assigned or could find out myself. It was hard work and you never knew what the day had in store when you woke up in the morning. One day you could be sent to cover a fire at the local cinema and the next you would be sent to report on the opening of a new bakery.

My first experience of reporting on anything to do with football was when I went to work for the *Johnstone Advertiser*. The *Advertiser* covered a patch that included St Mirren, and their manager at the time was a man called Alex Ferguson. When I was sent to their training ground for the first time, I tried to make a good impression by introducing myself to the manager.

'Mr Ferguson, I'm pleased to meet you,' I said. 'I'm Jim White from the *Advertiser*. I won't keep you long.'

'You're dead right you won't keep me long,' Ferguson said as he walked away.

After that false start, I think I ended up getting as close as any journalist could get to Sir Alex during his incredible career. When I saw him recently, I mentioned our first meeting. He couldn't remember it at all – why would he? – but we did have a good laugh about it.

One of the moments my life really changed was in 1979 when I was just twenty-one and I saw an advert in the *Glasgow Herald*. STV were looking for a news reporter to work on the nightly *Scotland Today* programme and I decided to apply. They wrote back to offer me an interview and I must have said the right things because I got the job. It felt incredible to be given such an opportunity at such a young age, but they didn't just pluck me out of thin air. Even though I was only twenty-one, I was a qualified journalist with experience of working in local newspapers. If I hadn't got that job, there's a pretty good chance I would never have ended up having such a long career in broadcasting. It was exciting and daunting at the same time because I had never been on TV before and I didn't really know what to expect.

Looking back, perhaps I shouldn't have worried too much, because working in TV news in those days was a real thrill. We are talking about a time before the internet, social media and satellite and cable TV. There were only about three TV channels and everyone seemed to watch the same programmes. My working days were even more exciting than they had been at local papers. I was covering the same kinds of stories – crime and human interest – but everything just felt a little bit more glamorous. In those days, we shot everything on 16mm film and we had to send it to a laboratory north of Glasgow for it to be processed before we could start editing it. *Scotland Today* was on every weekday at 6 p.m. so it was a real rush to get everything ready in time, and sometimes the pictures would go out live while you read out your script over them in an edit suite.

For a young reporter like me, Glasgow felt like the centre of the world and it was what, in those days, you would call 'a happening city'. I loved my job and I really wanted to make my mark. To do that, I decided I would need to stop relying on my producers to assign stories to me. What I needed to do was come up with my own original material. I figured that the best way of doing that would be to get interviews with the big stars who would regularly come to perform in Glasgow.

In those days, all the big acts would play at the Apollo Theatre, so I decided that would be the place to target for my move into entertainment and showbusiness journalism. I would read all the papers and look out for flyers to see who was coming to town, and if they were playing at the Apollo I would head there with a cameraman and wait for the stars to appear.

That's how I ended up having a memorable encounter with Mick Jagger. The Rolling Stones were playing at the Apollo so my cameraman and I had spent the day waiting in a lane at the side of the venue by the stage door. In my head

I was singing the chorus of one of my favourite Stones songs, 'You Can't Always Get What You Want'. If you like the Stones, you will know that the song goes on to advise that if you try sometimes, you might get what you need.

Sure enough, after a few hours I did get what I needed because a car pulled up and there was a big commotion as Jagger and Jerry Hall got out with their security guards.

'Mick, how are you? Can I grab a quick word?'

The two of them disappeared inside the venue before I had even finished speaking. I think I was in a state of shock at just having seen one of the most famous men in the world and one of my musical heroes. Maybe that was the reason I stayed where I was instead of going back to the office, or maybe it was because I thought I would try and get another member of the Stones arriving. Whatever the reason, it paid off, because soon after one of Jagger's minders came out and said, 'Come in and you can have five minutes with Mick,' which goes to show that sometimes you really can get what you want and what you need.

Not for the first or last time I had talked myself into an incredible situation and not for the first or last time I didn't know what to say. You see, even at that young age I had developed a bit of a reputation for myself as someone who was decent at getting his foot in the door and getting interviews – but what happened next wasn't always as polished as it should have been.

One of the secrets of getting a good interview is doing your research and preparation, but in those days I was just taking a chance on getting someone famous to talk. I was running around after any celebrity who came to Glasgow, and as I was spending most of my time out and about, and there were no laptops or smartphones, I didn't really have much time to prepare properly. I was hanging around on the street waiting, I wasn't at the local library or leafing through the newspaper archives doing my research. No one had even thought of the internet and search engines back then, so it was just me, a cameraman and a few ideas for questions in the little notebooks I carried around with me at all times.

I was starstruck and unprepared as I was led through the stage door of the Apollo for a brief audience with the one and only Mick Jagger. I don't remember much about the interview except that Jagger was very friendly and charming, even when I asked him why tickets for the show were so expensive at six pounds each. The booking fee on a ticket to see the Stones is probably more than six pounds now.

After Jagger, I was on a roll and I felt like I could get every big star who set foot in Scotland. In 1983, David Bowie was top of the charts all over the world with 'Let's Dance', and it was announced that he would be playing at Murrayfield in Edinburgh in June as part of his *Serious Moonlight* world tour. I'm not quite sure how I did it, but I managed to get in touch with his management company and convinced them to let me interview Bowie on the day of the show. I thought I was dreaming when I ended up sitting in front of Bowie with the camera rolling.

He was one of the biggest stars in the world, another one of my musical heroes, a man who was style and sophistication personified, whereas I was just a TV reporter with a mullet and a moustache. He must have come across thousands of reporters like me during his career, but he was incredibly accommodating, polite and charming, sitting there looking like a million dollars in his powder blue suit. I thought I'd better start off by asking him how long we would have. 'Don't worry,' he said. 'Just start.'

I was flying by this stage of my career and I was so confident I even thought I could interview the most famous ballet dancer in the world. What could possibly go wrong?

To cut a long story short, Rudolf Nureyev was appearing at the Edinburgh Festival at the Usher Hall. I knew absolutely nothing about ballet but that wasn't going to stand in the way of my determination to get an interview with him, even though it was well known that he hardly ever spoke to journalists. Nureyev liked to let his dancing do the talking but that was no good to me. I had to get him to talk and I somehow managed to find out that he was staying at Edinburgh's Caledonian Hotel.

You can guess what happened next. Yours truly went and stood outside the hotel all day with a cameraman and waited for the great man to emerge. Sure enough, after a few hours, Nureyev appeared in a great big grey coat and a knitted hat.

'Mr Nureyev, I'm Jim White from STV. Can I have a quick word?'

Before I knew it, Nureyev was in the back of a limousine being driven off. Now I may not have known exactly where he was going but I did know where he might be going. I jumped in my car with the cameraman and we screeched off towards the Usher Hall. There wasn't much traffic in those days, so we got there pretty quickly and waited outside. A few minutes later, the limousine arrived and Nureyev got out.

'Mr Nureyev, I'm Jim White from STV. Can I have a quick word?'

I think Nureyev either took pity on me or was impressed by my tenacity and perseverance. Well, I know it was a mix of the two because he told me. He said he was so impressed I could come inside and interview him, as long as I didn't take up too much of his time because he had to rehearse for his big show.

Before I knew it, I was backstage standing in front of one of the world's most famous ballet dancers. It should have been one of the crowning glories of my career but, unfortunately, I was not as well prepared as I should have been.

Nureyev began by explaining politely that he very rarely spoke to the media. I started off by asking him what he thought of Edinburgh. I think my second, third and fourth questions were about Edinburgh as well. He was charismatic and very accommodating, even though I think he realised pretty quickly I was out of my depth. When the interview was over, we said our goodbyes and his publicist came over to show us out. I will never forget what he said as we left. 'That was fascinating, Mr White. It is the first interview Rudolf has ever done without ballet being mentioned!'

To tell you the truth, by that stage of my career I was already aware of the fact that I was better at getting interviews than doing them. But I was still young and I had time to learn, and my bosses were delighted that I was getting all these big names to talk to me.

Maybe I am being too hard on myself criticising the quality of those interviews, because it's not as if they were in-depth, one-hour specials, they were just the fruits of a young reporter going out there and doing his very best. I was thinking on my feet and living on my wits, I was backing myself and taking risks, I had bags of enthusiasm and drive. Looking back, I know now that you can be the best interviewer in the world but if you lack that tenacity and perseverance you are going to end up interviewing an empty chair – unless you have bookers and producers getting you your guests.

To be a good interviewer, you have to be a good listener. You have to listen carefully to every answer and pick up on anything interesting that is said and ask follow-up questions. One of the mistakes you can make when you are interviewing someone is to just go through lists of questions. If you simply stick to your list of questions and don't listen to the answers, you are not engaging with your subject and there will be no connection between you – and that's where some of the best responses come from. I like to think that I have got better at interviewing as I have got older, but it is a lot tougher than it looks. Just a few days ago, I was invited to a central London hotel and told I could have ten minutes with a Premier League club owner. Ten minutes is not a lot of time and certainly not enough to ask all the questions I wanted to ask, a lot of them on behalf of his club's supporters, but what could I do? The interview was being done on his terms and there was no room for negotiation. I could take it or leave it.

I'm not making excuses. Interviewing people is a difficult art to master and, even at my ripe old age, I am learning all the time. Back in the eighties, I knew that I had done very well to get interviews with real stars like Jagger, Bowie and Nureyev. I was elated heading back to the office with my exclusives, but deep down I knew I had been a little bit overawed by those experiences. I was talking, they were talking and I was listening, but I should have been more confident and I should have listened more.

I was definitely listening more by the time I managed to interview Brian Clough at Glasgow airport when Nottingham Forest came to play Celtic in the UEFA Cup in December 1983. It was never a good idea to interrupt Clough and at that stage of my career I was more than happy to let him do all the talking. I also managed to get the great Johan Cruyff at Glasgow airport and it was beginning to dawn on me, and my bosses, that I was feeling more at home in the world of football than the world of culture and entertainment.

Another really big turning point in my life was in 1986, when I was sent to cover Scotland at the World Cup in Mexico. It was incredible to be a small part of such a major tournament and reporting on your country at a World Cup is one of the best experiences I have had during my career. I was there when Scotland played well but lost 1–0 to Denmark in their opening game, and it was the same story again when West Germany won 2–1 after Gordon Strachan had put Scotland ahead. That meant Scotland had to win their final group game against Uruguay. Unfortunately, they just couldn't score against their tough-tackling and no-nonsense opponents, even after José Batista was sent off for a disgraceful tackle on Gordon Strachan after just fifty-six seconds.

Scotland were going home and so was I, after an incredible experience which wasn't totally ruined by the fact that my team finished bottom of their group. A Scotland supporter called Munro summed up what it all meant when he told me he had sold his house to finance his trip of a lifetime to Mexico. 'Does your wife know you sold her house?' I asked him. 'Not yet,' he said. 'She will in the fullness of time.'

Interviewing a member of the public is called a vox pop in journalism. It comes from the Latin phrase *vox populi*, which means 'voice of the people'. Some reporters dread being sent to a high street or a football match to interview strangers, but I have no problem speaking to anyone, anywhere, any time. I have always thought that to be a good reporter, you have to be able to get on with people. You have to be interested in other people, in their lives and stories.

If you can't get on with people then it is going to be almost impossible for you to break a story or get a big interview. The only way you are going to get a big football story is if you speak to people. The more people you know in football and the more you stay in touch and speak to them, the more likely it is that you are going to get good stories. You are not going to break any transfer stories if you don't have good relationships with agents, players, managers, owners and club executives – and if they are not comfortable knowing and speaking to you.

Luckily for me, I have always loved meeting people. I love getting in front of them and speaking to them and, like every journalist, I love getting a good story. I love it because it is my job and I like being good at my job. Deep down, I suppose we all also want some praise and recognition. I think the person I was trying to impress most in my younger days was my father, Robbie. He is the one who instilled a love of football in me by taking me to so many games, and he would be absolutely delighted that during my career I have had the chance to go to so many incredible games and meet and interview so many extraordinary players and managers.

People sometimes ask me if I get nervous before interviews or before meeting a famous player or manager. I suppose the truth is sometimes I do a little bit. Like many people, I try to hide that and overcome it with my natural confidence and positive attitude. Apart from my invaluable journalism diploma, I have never had any training on how to present on TV or radio. I know what you're thinking – It shows, Jim!

In all honesty, I have never had any hints or tips on how to present. You just have to do your best to relax and be yourself. If you do that, people are either going to like you or they're not and if you are lucky there will be more of the former than the latter.

Of course, I occasionally get feedback from the people I work for, but no one has ever told me I am sensationally good and no one has ever told me that I should give up and try something else. As you get older, you realise that you know yourself if something has gone well – you don't necessarily need anyone else to tell you that you have done a good job. How many times does a bus driver get a pat on the back? How often do teachers get praised by their heads? I am no different, I am just doing a job and I always try to do it to the best of my ability.

One of the real thrills of my job is reporting live on stories, especially transfer stories. I've lost count of the number of times a big story is breaking and I am live on TV or radio, at the same time as I am messaging contacts to try and get the very latest information. One of the best times to get in touch with contacts is during ad breaks, when you have two or three minutes to make a quick call or send a couple of messages. I have always thought that I would have found it difficult to work at somewhere like the BBC where they don't have any ad breaks. I need those short breaks to get new lines and develop the big stories. That immediacy is what makes the job exciting and that is what people want – to be the first to hear something they don't already know.

I always try to get to know new faces in English football as quickly as possible. During the World Cup in Qatar, I was lucky enough to be a guest for a game in the same executive box as Todd Boehly, the American businessman who had led the consortium which had bought Chelsea from Roman Abramovich for £2.5 billion in May 2022.

Getting to know Boehly proved to be very helpful in the January 2023 window when Chelsea spent an astonishing £323 million on new players. The new Chelsea owners have been heavily criticised for the vast amount of money they have spent on transfers and for the way they have run the club. I know for a fact that they are aware of all the criticism and they take it to heart. In April 2023, it emerged that Chelsea co-owners Boehly and Behdad Eghbali had gone into the home dressing room after a 2–1 home defeat by Brighton at Stamford Bridge to speak to the players. It is an unwritten rule of the game that owners should only really go in the dressing room after a big result like a cup win. Boehly and Eghbali have their own way of doing things and I think they were surprised by the backlash about what they had done.

There are two sides to every story. On the one hand, you can see why some supporters were unhappy about the owners taking such a hands-on approach, but on the other hand, you could argue that going into the dressing room showed how much they cared. I think Boehly and Eghbali wanted to speak to the players on behalf of the Chelsea fans who spend so much money and give up so much of their time to follow their team home and away. There was nothing malicious or sinister about what they did, they just wanted to tell the players they had to fight and give everything when they played for Chelsea. Personally, I don't have a problem with it as long as it is done in moderation. After all, you wouldn't want your owners going into the dressing room after every game.

One transfer deal I will never forget involved Alex Oxlade-Chamberlain on deadline day in the summer of 2017. His Arsenal contract was running out, he was in demand and lots of people were reporting that he was on his way to Chelsea. Luckily, I had a good contact close to the player and when it mattered he gave me the information I needed. He told me to forget about Chelsea because the player only wanted to sign for Liverpool. That's what I reported and sure enough a few hours later he signed for Liverpool in a £35 million deal.

I have to admit, when I am driving home on nights like that, I sometimes think about the old days when I was starting out at STV. In those days the autocue we used looked like something that had been typed up on toilet paper for us to read, and if they wanted to make any changes to the scripts they had to get the scissors out and cut out the paragraphs they didn't want and then stick it all back together with Sellotape. Despite all that, I still have some fantastic memories of those days and I wouldn't change them for the world.

Nowadays we have state-of-the-art autocues and laptops and tablets, but I like to ad-lib as much as possible because I want to engage the audience and make them feel part of the conversation. You can't always do that if you just stick to the script. You also have to amplify your voice a little bit when you are broadcasting and you have to be on the front foot and switched on but all that comes pretty naturally to me.

This is just the way I am, it is the way I have always been and I am sure you won't be surprised to hear that I have never had any voice coaching or elocution lessons. I am afraid to say what you see is most definitely what you get as far as I am concerned.

Of course, when you are broadcasting, live things can and often do go wrong. The best way to deal with it is to make light of it. You don't want to panic, because if you do it will unsettle the viewers and listeners. If something goes wrong, just move on to the next item, it's not a big deal, keep things in perspective at all times and try and laugh and joke about it.

Some people say you should always watch yourself back on TV or listen back to your shows. They say that is the only way you can improve, by looking back and seeing how and where you can improve next time. Looking and listening back is something I hardly ever do. As soon as a show is over I am thinking about the next one. I don't need to watch or listen back to something to know whether it has gone well or not. My mindset is that I have to keep moving on, I have to make tomorrow's show even better than today's show, I have to get more stories and more interviews, I have to give my audience what they want again and again and again – until they've had enough of me!

Being a good journalist is what really drives me. I have always been driven, but not to be successful. I think I have been driven to be accepted. I want people to think I am a good journalist and a good broadcaster and I want people to enjoy my shows. I want to be accepted by the viewers and the listeners and my colleagues.

If you want to get in this business just to be rich or famous then you are going to be disappointed. Fame in whatever shape or form is not going to make you happier, it is not going to make you feel better about yourself, and that is coming from someone who doesn't even consider themselves to be famous.

Whatever small amount of fame I may have comes from the fact that I spend my life talking about football, something that millions and millions of people all around the world are passionate about. I was in South Africa a few years ago for a holiday and I got in a taxi at Cape Town airport. Straight away I could see the driver was staring at me in his rear-view mirror when his eyes weren't on the road. 'Where is the yellow tie? You are the transfer man!' he said as we headed towards my hotel.

The yellow tie tag follows me everywhere even though I stopped wearing one years ago. My actual yellow tie from all those deadline days is now in the National Football Museum in Manchester next to one of John Motson's signature sheepskin coats. I am told it is still a very popular exhibit and it was a real thrill to hand over the tie in person to the museum.

It's funny and touching that I – and my yellow tie – have become so synonymous with transfers and deadline days. I think there were a few years when people even started to wear yellow ties to work on deadline days as a way of sharing in the fun and excitement.

It's not always easy broadcasting live for hours and hours when you have something tied around your neck, but even though everyone seems to dress much more casually these days, I always thought a suit and tie gives you real authority and gravitas on air.

I have to let you in on a secret, though. At this precise moment in time I don't own a single yellow tie.

Chapter 3

How the Hell Did You Get My Number?

There is only one way to get a transfer story and that is to use your contacts. If you don't have contacts you are wasting your time in this business. People often make the mistake of thinking you have to be a fantastic writer to make it as a sports journalist. Don't get me wrong, being a good writer helps, but what really counts is your ability to get stories.

Speak to anyone in a senior position in journalism and they will tell you there are lots of people who can write well and you can find them everywhere. Finding someone who can get you stories is much more difficult. If you can do both, then great, you are going to have a long and rewarding career, because what editors want more than anything else is stories, they don't want 1,000 words of flowery prose or opinion. They have lots of people who can give them that. In my experience, you can be a very average writer, but as long as you can get stories you will always have a job.

There are still lots of very talented sub-editors out there

– although not as many as there used to be because of all the cuts in the newspaper industry – who will turn your turgid prose into readable copy. They won't mind doing it if you have a story, but if you can't get them a story, you may as well give up now, no matter how good a writer you are. The only way to get stories is to go to as many games as possible, as many events as possible, introduce yourself, speak to people, be polite and engaging and close the deal by getting their number.

It's not easy and you have to have a certain amount of front and a thick skin to do it, but you have nothing to lose. What is the worst thing that can happen? They say they don't want to give you their number. So what? What have you lost? Nothing. At least you tried and more often than not, you will get the number.

I remember a colleague once asked José Mourinho for his number after waiting for him for hours outside his house. José said, 'No. Give me your number.' Now, you would think that was José brushing him off and letting him down gently, but a few minutes later my colleague got a message on his phone. It wasn't just from anyone either. He now had José's number.

It can be nerve-wracking asking people for their number, but you just have to summon up the courage and do it, otherwise you are wasting your time trying to make a name for yourself in this industry. My advice is always be polite and introduce yourself and engage with whoever you are speaking to. Don't just rush into asking for a number because you are not going to get it that way. You have to make conversation and establish a rapport and, when you get a chance, just say it would be good to stay in touch and ask if you can exchange numbers.

Graeme Souness is someone I would now call a friend. He has been so good to me over many years. The only reason I know him at all is because I asked him for his number back in the eighties when he was on international duty for Scotland in Glasgow. He was playing for Sampdoria at the time and living in Genoa. We got on so well that he invited me out to Italy to make a documentary about his life in Serie A. Some of the younger generation may not realise just how great a player Graeme was, and he has also always been an absolute gentleman – despite what some of his opponents might say. I still remember asking Graeme for his number and writing it down in my little notepad. Keep in mind, those were the days before mobile phones, so what I had was his home number in Italy. I couldn't text or message or email him – if I wanted to contact him I had to call and hope he was at home.

That one phone number and that special connection opened a lot of doors for me. I went out to Genoa to film the documentary about him for STV and he made sure we got incredible access, not just to him but everyone at the club, including his teammate Trevor Francis. I will never forget being on the Sampdoria team coach with Graeme and him pointing to two youngsters who were laughing and joking. 'Look out for them,' Graeme said. 'They can play.'

He was not wrong. Those two men were Gianluca Vialli and Roberto Mancini.

The reaction to the documentary was very good when it was shown in Scotland and I stayed in touch with Graeme. I think he liked and trusted me, especially because one Friday night in 1986 he called me and provided me with another of my life-changing moments. There had been some speculation that Jock Wallace would be leaving Rangers for the second time after coming back to manage the club again in 1983. I will never forget what Graeme told me on the phone from Italy that night.

'Try and keep this to yourself. You are speaking to the next player-manager of Rangers. I'm coming to a charity night in Glasgow next week.'

To say I was shocked would be an understatement. I was speechless and, because I was just a young, inexperienced reporter, I didn't do anything or tell anyone for three days. On Monday, I went into the office and told my bosses and then I went to Glasgow airport to get shots of Graeme arriving. He was flying in via London Heathrow and I made sure we got the shots before I went back to the studio to go on set at 6 p.m. to talk about this big story.

In time, Graeme became one of my best contacts, but it would be wrong to assume that our relationship has just been transactional. The best contacts are also friends and that's what Graeme and I became over the years. He has always gone out of his way to help me when he can.

For instance, I am thinking of the times he tipped me off that Rangers were signing Terry Butcher and Mark Hateley, or when he let me have an exclusive interview with Mark Walters when he was signed from Aston Villa in 1987 and became the first black player to play for Rangers.

Graeme also gave me the inside track in 1989, when former Celtic forward Mo Johnston made headlines all over the world by becoming the most high-profile Roman Catholic to sign for Rangers. Graeme let us film Johnston in the Ibrox dressing room and he also arranged for us to interview him. 'Don't go crazy,' Graeme said, and if my memory serves me well I followed his instructions and wrapped the interview up after about ten minutes. I wasn't going to push my luck. I had a big interview in the bag thanks to Graeme.

We are still friends more than thirty years later and I'm absolutely delighted that we get to work together on talk-SPORT as well. Of course, it all started back in the eighties. It began with a young, inexperienced reporter taking a deep breath and summoning up the courage to ask Graeme for his number.

Players, agents and managers are great contacts to have and you can't beat getting to know a club owner, either. When Farhad Moshiri was starting to get involved at Everton, one of his colleagues gave me his number and said Farhad might want to talk to me. I introduced myself by text and, when we were both at Stamford Bridge watching Chelsea beat Everton 5–0 in 2016, I texted him asking for his box number. After the game, I went up to see him.

There was a lot of security there, but when I got in Farhad walked towards me to welcome me and introduced me to someone he called his friend – Alisher Usmanov. Looking back, it may have been one of the few occasions when I was slightly lost for words. In any case, if I'd had my wits about me I would have asked Usmanov for his number, but for whatever reason – it may have been the security or the mood in the box after Everton had lost so heavily – I didn't have the courage to just go ahead and ask him. I did manage to get it later, but that is another story.

As far as Farhad is concerned, I have to say I like him as a person. I think he has had honourable intentions at Everton but the way things have turned out has been far from satisfactory. I totally understand the strength of feeling among the Everton fans about what has happened to their club and I would feel exactly the same way if I was one of them.

There is a fair amount of ill feeling towards me from Everton fans because of my relationship with Farhad but, as far as I am concerned, it is nothing personal. Everton are one of the biggest clubs in the world and they have an incredible history. I have nothing but respect for the club and their fans. At the end of the day, I am just trying to do my job to the best of my abilities and an important part of my job is getting to know the people who own and run clubs. It is as simple as that.

When there were stories flying around that Everton were considering making Rafa Benítez their manager in 2021, I called Farhad to see if I could find out what was going on. Of course, appointing Benítez was going to be very controversial because he had managed Liverpool for six years and reportedly called Everton 'a small club' after a goalless draw in a Merseyside derby in 2007.

I think Farhad was in a restaurant in Italy when I called, but he agreed to give me a quick interview on the phone and he confirmed that Benítez was going to be the next Everton manager after Carlo Ancelotti. I asked Farhad if he had any reservations about Benítez's past. Farhad said he had weighed everything up and he was convinced that he was getting the best man available for the job. 'Rafa is not in love with Liverpool,' Farhad said. 'He is in love with the city of Liverpool.'

I think some of the adverse publicity surrounding my relationship with Farhad is the reason why I am not in touch with him that much these days. Owners know what they are letting themselves in for when they buy clubs. There is always going to be scrutiny and they have to expect a rough ride if things are not going well on the pitch. Sometimes it feels like they are in a lose-lose situation, because if they never talk to the media they are accused of being silent and unaccountable, but when they do talk, they are accused of creating headlines and rocking the boat.

Owners are often the best contacts to have when it comes to breaking transfer stories, because they are the ones signing

47

the cheques and they are the ones who ultimately decide whether a player is going to be bought or sold. Of course, they can't say anything that would jeopardise a potential deal, but they like to help out when they can and Farhad was good enough to point me in the right direction when Everton bought and sold players such as Wayne Rooney and Michael Keane. The turnover of players has been so high at Everton in recent times that it would have been impossible for me to have the inside track on every deal. Farhad occasionally guided me when he could and on one memorable occasion he even agreed to give me a quick phone interview about Ross Barkley as he was walking out of an opera in the south of France.

By the way, that was Farhad and not Ross walking out of the opera. I know Ross played for Nice and lived in the south of France but I am not sure he is a big fan of *Carmen* or *The Marriage of Figaro*. Seriously though, I have always got on well with Farhad and I have a lot of respect for him. But maybe he was not prepared for owning such a big club in a game where passions run so high.

My friendship with Farhad started with me getting his number and the same thing happened with the former Southampton chief executive, Nicola Cortese. You are not always going to get an opportunity to meet someone face-to-face to try and get their number. Sometimes your paths have not crossed and sometimes they just say 'No' when you ask. I never take it personally when someone doesn't give me their number. If you don't ask you don't get and if you don't get you just have to find another way of getting what you want. If they say 'No' I get it from someone else.

I had never met Cortese when I managed to get his number in 2009. I wanted it because he had become executive chairman of Southampton and they were on the up and he seemed to be a very interesting character – an outsider in English football who had been working as a banker in Switzerland. As soon as I got his number, I texted him and he called me back. That is one of the benefits of being on TV or radio or writing for a newspaper – if you have a relatively high profile and people are aware of you, they are much more likely to call back. In a sense, if they call you back it might mean they already like you without having met you in person.

We got on well on the phone and Nicola invited me to be his guest at St Mary's for a Southampton game. I can't remember much about the game, but I do remember the time Nicola called and asked me if I wanted to go to Barcelona with him to meet the next Southampton manager. That is how I managed to get an interview with Mauricio Pochettino and little did I know that he was going to turn out to be such a fantastic manager.

Nicola was a very interesting character and he liked to do things his own way. Southampton had very good players like Adam Lallana in those days which must have made his job easier. It is a shame he is not working in football but we are still in touch and I think he still has a lot to offer the game.

It can be difficult to have personal relationships with people in football when you are a journalist but that doesn't mean you shouldn't try. They may be wary of you to begin with, but over time you can get over that and gain their trust. At the end of the day, you want information and access and the only way you are going to get that is if you get numbers and get to know people. There is absolutely no excuse for not trying to build up your contacts. I have something like two thousand numbers stored on my phone and I still have two Filofaxes somewhere with some incredible numbers for players, managers and agents going back forty years.

I sometimes get asked for advice by youngsters who are starting out in sports journalism and I always tell them the most important thing is to make contacts. I'm not suggesting that a young journalist new to the job marches up to Pep Guardiola or Lionel Messi and asks for their number. That's not the way it works. You have to start at the bottom and work your way up. A lot of the best reporters in this business started out working in local papers and nothing can beat that as a foundation for a long and successful career in journalism. It is just a real shame that so many local papers have closed down and the ones that are left are often a poor imitation of what they used to be, because of massive cuts to budgets and resources and the ubiquity of the internet and social media.

I am not sure I had even heard of social media when I first got to know Jonathan Barnett. He represents some of the best players in the world and I was in regular contact with him in 2013 when Gareth Bale's potential move from Tottenham Hotspur to Real Madrid dominated the headlines in the summer window. The transfer eventually went through for £85 million and, as always, I tried to make sure I was at the heart of the story.

I managed to get through to Jonathan the day before the deal was done and he let me know that everything had been verbally agreed. This was the biggest transfer story of the summer and I wanted to make sure I had as much exclusive material as possible. Even though it was a Sunday, I managed to convince Jonathan to let me go to his offices near Hyde Park to interview him and his business partner, David Manasseh. Once the interview was in the bag, Jonathan and David told me they were going to Luton airport to get on a private jet to Madrid with Gareth Bale. That news was like a red rag to a bull.

'Great! I'm coming with you,' I said, as it dawned on me that I didn't have my passport. Thankfully, they let me get in the car to the airport with them and on the way I got on my phone to arrange for a cameraman to meet me there. I could see Jonathan and David were getting a little bit concerned. There they were, trying to do the deal of the summer, an incredible, world record deal involving one of the biggest clubs in the world buying one of the best young players in the world – and there was yours truly right in the centre of the action.

Unfortunately, I couldn't talk my way on to the plane but

I did give it a good go – despite not having my passport. Of course, I know how the game works and Jonathan and David explained to me that they were under strict orders that Gareth was not to speak to anyone until he was unveiled at his official Real Madrid presentation. I had to respect their wishes because they had given me so much already, even though it wasn't everything I wanted. I didn't get on the plane and I didn't get a sit-down interview with Gareth. But I was pretty happy on the train home. I had got the inside track on the deal of the summer, interviews with the agents involved, shots of Gareth leaving the UK and a few words from him as well.

In a perfect world you would always be breaking big transfer stories which come out of nowhere. The truth of the matter, though, is that it is extremely difficult to do this on a consistent basis. There are so many stories out there now that a lot of the moves are telegraphed months in advance. So what you want to work towards is being in a position where your contacts are so good that there is always someone you can get in touch with when there is a big story developing. As a reporter, you will only ever be as good as the people you know.

In April 2021, it emerged that twelve of the biggest clubs in Europe had signed up to form a Super League. It was such a big story that it was front and back page news. I needed to get a respected voice on to my radio show at short notice and luckily I had Arsène Wenger's number. He was working at FIFA so it might not have been easy for him to talk but I managed to convince him to come on. He was brilliant at explaining just why the breakaway plans were so divisive. The response to that show was incredible, with Arsène and Simon Jordan dissecting and debating one of the biggest football stories ever.

Wenger, along with Sir Alex Ferguson, has been one of the towering managers of the modern era in English football. Despite getting to know Sir Alex pretty well over the years, his phone numbers have been a closely guarded secret and I have never had them. I have always had to go through his son, Jason, to get in touch with Sir Alex, whereas things have been a little bit easier with his great Arsenal rival.

I actually had to wait quite a while to get Arsène's number. I only managed to get it when David Seaman announced he was retiring and I wanted to get his former manager to pay tribute to him. That just goes to prove that if you are persistent you will usually end up getting what you want. People in football are often wary about giving their numbers out but they realise that the media is a big part of the game now, and it benefits them in the long run to have good relationships with journalists.

Referees are different. They don't have to talk to anybody, at least until they retire. Quite a few of them are carving out a lucrative career in the media these days, especially now that the introduction of VAR has led to so many more talking points surrounding key decisions. The most famous referee in the world is arguably Pierluigi Collina. He retired from refereeing in 2005 and he now works for FIFA and has become a little more open when it comes to dealing with the media. So much so that when the twentieth anniversary of Manchester United's astonishing comeback win over Bayern Munich in the 1999 Champions League final came around, I decided to call him to see if he would talk to me about his memories of that night.

'Hi Pierluigi. It's Jim White here. I just wanted to see if I could talk to you about the 1999 Champions League final?'

That is as far as I got because Collina put the phone down on me. To be fair, he did answer when I called him back soon after. He apologised for putting the phone down on me and he explained that I had called him in the middle of his daily run. He was also kind enough to give me a few words about his memories of the Nou Camp in 1999.

You have to be prepared for things going wrong when you call contacts – especially when you are getting in touch for the first time. I had a memorable encounter with the Thai businessman Dejphon Chansiri after he bought Sheffield Wednesday in 2015. I called him and introduced myself as soon as he picked up the phone. I could tell straight away that there was something wrong.

'How did you get my number?' he said. 'How did you get my number?'

He was not happy. He kept asking me the same question over and over again. He was very insistent that he absolutely had to know who had given it to me. There was no way I was going to tell him. Eventually he accepted defeat and I think he respected me for that in a strange kind of way because we've gone on to have a pretty good relationship.

I was delighted for Chansiri when I saw him at the League One play-off final at Wembley in May 2023. Sheffield Wednesday had just beaten Barnsley to win promotion to the Championship and I saw Chansiri deep in thought while his fellow club directors were celebrating. I managed to speak to him after the game and after I had congratulated him, he explained that there were no hard feelings about me ringing him out of the blue all those years ago.

'Honestly, Jim,' he said. 'I wasn't angry that you called me, I just don't like receiving calls from anonymous numbers.'

One of the kindest, nicest and most helpful men I ever met in the game was the former Newcastle United chairman Freddy Shepherd. I had interviewed him a few times but little did I know that he was going to help provide me with one of the most memorable experiences of my career.

In August 2005, Newcastle signed the England number nine, Michael Owen, from Real Madrid for £17 million. Freddy kindly invited me to his unveiling ceremony at St James' Park. Not only that, but on the day he also asked me to go on stage and interview Michael live on TV in front of a sea of tens of thousands of fans.

I will never forget his words to me before the interview: 'Get on that stage, Jim, and give the fans what they want.' That is exactly what I tried to do and it was an incredible thrill and an experience I will never forget.

Freddy was a great contact and a fantastic man. He even organised an exclusive interview for me with legendary Newcastle and England manager Sir Bobby Robson. Shepherd was a passionate Geordie and he was sensitive and fun at the same time. He sadly passed away in 2017. He was the best of company.

It's not all plain sailing when it comes to contacts and not everyone wants to talk or have a relationship with the media. All you can do is respect their wishes when they make that clear. Over the years, I have tried to get Tottenham Hotspur executive chairman Daniel Levy to give me an interview but he always turns me down politely by explaining that's not the way he does things. You never know, though, I will keep trying and perhaps one day he will change his mind.

Just once in a while, fate gives you a helping hand and you end up making a good contact totally by chance. Back in 1994, I was living in Glasgow's southside but I was looking to move and I had put my flat on the market. One day, the estate agent called and told me he had someone interested in the property and I might know him.

I ended up selling the flat to Fergus McCann, the Scottish-Canadian businessman who had just bought a controlling stake in Celtic. I'm not sure he would have bought it off me if he had known about my Rangers connections.

Having said that, he must have liked me and the flat because I got to know him over the years and he was always good to me. He was frank and honest and always did what he said he was going to do.

I often wonder how much the flat is worth now. My only regret is I didn't bug it before I moved out. Only joking.

Chapter 4

Tony Blair 2 Gordon Brown 1

If you believe what some people write on social media, there are journalists out there who just make up transfer stories. In this parallel universe, reporters wake up in the morning, switch on their laptops and just write whatever they want. There are also people on social media who are convinced that there are reporters who have an agenda against the team they support.

I have never met a football reporter who makes up stories or one who has it in for a particular team. I think it's important that we make that clear. I know lots of journalists and what they are interested in is doing their job to the best of their abilities to make sure that they keep getting paid at the end of every month.

There have been big cuts and job losses across the media industry for as long as I can remember. Sports journalism is a very difficult profession to get into. You have to keep performing to keep your job because there is an army of younger and cheaper talent just waiting for an opportunity to take your place.

If you make up stories – or have an agenda against particular teams – you will lose your job very quickly. Being a football reporter is not as glamorous as many people think. It is a tough job and it has become even tougher in the past twenty years. The days of just having to write for the next day's paper are long gone. The modern football reporter has to write for his website, his paper and social media and increasingly he's been asked to film videos of himself summing up games and big stories.

And it's not just footballers who are being pushed to the limit by being made to play more and more games; there are reporters out there who are now covering about a hundred games a season. I know one reporter who regularly drives fifty thousand miles a season going to games, press conferences and interviews. Reporters usually get to games hours before kick-off and leave long after the final whistle. On top of all the match reports, previews, interviews and features they write, they also have to find and write news stories and they are increasingly being asked to go on TV and radio as well to raise their profile and the profile of the paper or website they work for.

Making up stories and having an agenda is not an option. Keeping your job is all that matters and your prospects of doing that depend solely on how you perform day in, day out. There is no hiding place. The fruits of your labour are published and broadcast for everyone to read, watch, listen to and have an opinion about. If what you produce isn't good enough, you will be out of a job before you know it.

The best way to keep your job is to keep getting stories. Stories are what really matters. A big story used to sell papers and now it delivers more clicks and viewers and listeners. A sports editor will always prefer to get a short, punchy, exclusive news story saying, for example, that Manchester City have made a £200 million offer for Kylian Mbappé rather than a beautifully written 2,000-word feature on how crucial low blocks, transitions and counter-pressing have become in the modern game.

So, if stories are the most highly valued currency in football journalism, how do you go about getting one? How do you make sure that you are the first person who finds out and reports that City have made that blockbuster bid for Mbappé? Well, it's all about who you know and how much they like you and whether it's in their interest to tell you what you are trying to find out.

It's also about who you work for. The bigger and the more high-profile the organisation you work for, the more likely it is that people are going to want to speak to you and give you the information you want. If you telephone Mbappé's representatives, it is very unlikely they will pick up or respond to any of your messages or emails but if they are aware of you and your work and respect the outlet you work for, they just might get back to you.

They might not want to admit it in public but it suits people in the football business to have contacts in the media. Depending on how much they like you, these contacts may even end up being friends. Having contacts in the media helps players, managers, clubs and owners make sure their point of view or their side of a story is covered, and it can help in the long-term, too, because quite a few of these former players and managers want to work in the media when they retire.

It's impossible to get a transfer story if you don't know players, agents, managers and owners and it is relatively easy to spot the people on social media who pretend to be in the know in order to make a name for themselves and get more followers. Some people think it's easy to report on transfers because all you need to do is peddle rumours and speculation. Some people even call transfer news fake news. I hate that phrase. Just because a deal that has been reported doesn't happen doesn't mean it is fake news.

Deals fail to happen for lots of reasons and, in my experience, if a reporter says a club are interested in a player, it is because they have information from sources close to the player or the clubs involved who have given them that information. Of course, the reporter can't reveal their sources and their sources are not going to come out and back them up in public if people question their information. Being a transfer reporter can be a lonely business and sometimes you can feel very exposed. You just have to grin and bear it. It's all part of the job.

I've already mentioned Jack Grealish's £100 million move to Manchester City from Aston Villa and that is one of the transfers which involved me going out on a limb with the information that I was able to get. I reported on 25 June 2021 that Grealish would be leaving Villa and it was all but certain that he would be the subject of a huge bid which

Villa would find impossible not to accept. That did not go down well in some quarters and there were quite a few people who accused me of not knowing what I was talking about. I trusted my source so all I could do was sit tight. Six weeks later, Grealish moved to City after they triggered his release clause, but during those six weeks I did feel like I had been hung out to dry.

After my initial report, I had a message from a Villa source telling me in no uncertain terms that Grealish was central to their core objective of getting back into Europe, and it was already well known that both Manchester clubs and Tottenham Hotspur were interested in signing him. I was basically being told that the player was not for sale and he wasn't going anywhere. It was a polite way of telling me to keep quiet because I was wrong.

That didn't bother me. I know how the game works and I knew my information was right but there wasn't much I could do it about it. I just had to sit and wait and carry on doing my job. At that stage, the window was going to be open for another nine weeks so there was plenty of time for me to be proved right and, of course, there was plenty of time for me to take all sorts of abuse on social media from people who thought I was wrong. To be honest, the abuse doesn't bother me at all because I don't really take any notice of it. Anyway, Villa did get that huge offer which was impossible to turn down and Grealish did move. Did I brag about it? No, I just reported what I knew and what was happening. I got on with my job.

But you can't get every story right, and one which I got wrong was about the former Morocco centre-back, Medhi Benatia. In the summer of 2014, Benatia was a wanted man and it was thought Roma were prepared to listen to offers for him. Lots of big clubs wanted him, including Manchester United, and in the middle of August I got information from one of the biggest agents in the business that the player was indeed going to sign for United. On 16 August, I posted on Twitter that Benatia was 'on his way from AS Roma to Manchester United.'

Looking back, I should have chosen my words more carefully because Benatia never turned up in Manchester. As time went on, I became more crestfallen and I was taking a real battering on social media. The information came from a trusted and famous source who had never let me down before and I had checked it out with people I knew at United. They wanted to sign a centre-back and they were interested in the player. Unfortunately, it turned out to be an instance where I got ahead of myself; I shouldn't have made it look as if the player was definitely going to United. Eleven days later, Benatia signed for Bayern Munich in a €26 million deal and I got even more abuse on social media – most of it from angry United fans.

It didn't take me long to find out exactly what had happened behind the scenes. Benatia wanted to work with Pep Guardiola and Bayern Munich could offer him Champions League football. That was not on offer at United because they finished seventh at the end of the 2013–14 Premier League season.

I am not sure I will ever live down the Benatia episode but I am glad that most people seem to have forgotten about it now. It did teach me an important lesson about how carefully you have to choose your words on social media. The story did have a kind-of happy ending because I did eventually get to meet Benatia a few years later and talk to him about what went wrong for me and what might have been for him.

Thanks to my good friend and former colleague Kate Abdo, I was able to get a ticket for Bayern's home game against Bayer Leverkusen in December 2014. Before the game, I went to the club shop and bought a Bayern shirt with Benatia's name and number on the back. After the game, which Bayern won 1–0, I was hellbent on speaking to Benatia and I wasn't going to take 'No' for an answer. I managed to talk myself into a players' area near the dressing rooms in the Allianz Arena and I saw Benatia getting into a lift. It was now or never.

'Hi, Medhi. It's Jim White here from London. How are you enjoying life in Munich?'

We proceeded to have a very nice conversation and he confirmed that it had looked like he was going to Manchester United but then Bayern came in for him. I'm not making excuses here. I got it wrong and I hold my hands up. Having said that, it was nice to finally meet the man himself because he had been on my mind – and in my Twitter notifications – for six months. I'm not sure he realised how much grief he had caused me by signing for Bayern instead of United but there was really only one person to blame and that was me.

No journalist I know ever goes out to try and mislead people. Unfortunately, sometimes the goalposts can move and you can be left exposed. It's just one of the inherent risks of my job and it's a danger you are always looking out for and always trying to eliminate. Everybody makes mistakes, but if a journalist makes a mistake nowadays it's on social media and that means there is no hiding place. I own that mistake, there was no one to blame except me, but I do find it disappointing that so many people seem to delight in you getting something wrong. They really do seem to enjoy it and you feel like they are out there ready to pounce as soon as you make any kind of slip or mistake.

My tweet about Benatia was posted in August 2014, just eight months after I had joined Twitter. I was inexperienced and naive when it came to the dangers of social media. If I had posted that he 'could be on his way to United' instead of 'on his way' then I wouldn't have caused myself so many problems. You live and learn.

Although the information I had about United's serious interest in Benatia was right, there are other times when some of the more unscrupulous agents and middle-men involved in deals do lie to you. It's mostly done to generate interest in a player they represent or have a mandate to sell. They will call you and reel off a list of clubs who are interested in the player, and if you report what they have told you it could alert other clubs and increase the chances of a potential deal happening. Perhaps I'm being unfair by saying they lie, maybe it would be fairer to say they exaggerate and embellish in order to drum up interest. For instance, a scout from Manchester United may well have checked out a player but that does not necessarily mean United have any real interest in buying him.

As you get older and wiser, you realise what kind of information to trust and what information to be slightly sceptical about. You can't just rely on your instincts. You have to be guided by the track record of the people you are speaking to. If they are solid sources who represent players or work at a club, people who have never let you down in the past, then you are going to have more faith in what they are telling you. If they have fed you information in the past which turned out to be wide of the mark then you are naturally going to be much more cautious when they get back in touch. It's only natural, though, that agents want to get in touch with journalists. We seek access to them and they seek access to us. That's the way it works. After a while you know who to trust and who not to trust.

The people you have to be wary of are the people you have never dealt with before, the people who call you out of the blue and are evasive when you ask them how they got your number. A few years ago, one man called to tell me he had seen the Brazilian forward, Kaká, at Seven Sisters station, not far from Tottenham's ground, White Hart Lane. He was convinced Kaká was moving from Real Madrid to Spurs. When I told him I doubted it was Kaká and I doubted he would use the underground, he put the phone down on me.

I don't know a single journalist who would report something based on what a stranger had told them. Despite popular misconceptions, the vast majority of journalists are very honest, scrupulous and hard-working – the ones I know, in any case. I read a survey a few years ago which claimed it had found that journalists were the least trusted people in the UK after politicians. As far as I am concerned, the people who did that survey are the least trusted people in the UK.

I don't understand why journalists have such a bad reputation. Of course, there are bad apples in journalism like there are in any industry. There are good and bad people in every walk of life and journalism is no different. When it comes to the part of the business I know best, sports journalism, I have to say the standard in the UK is extremely high. I am proud to know some of the best sports journalists of this generation. They are people I look up to and admire and I am enormously flattered every now and then when they tell me they enjoy listening to my radio show.

I know some journalists used to look down their noses at sports journalists and maybe they still do. On some papers, people joked that the sports journalists worked in the toy department. No one has ever said anything like that to my face and I have never had an inferiority complex about what I do.

I have wondered sometimes whether I could have been successful in another part of this industry. For instance, could I have been a foreign reporter or present news bulletins? To tell you the truth, I don't see why not, although that's not to say I have any regrets. First and foremost, I am a journalist and I haven't spent my whole career covering sports.

My big break came when I got a job as a TV reporter and, after a few years, I specialised in sport. That's how I got my foot in the door and once I was in I was never going to let anyone throw me out. To make it in this industry you have to be like a player who will play in any position they are asked to play in by their manager. It's hard to get in the team and once you are in you have to do everything to keep your place. Going to the manager and asking to play somewhere else is probably just asking for trouble. I'm not sure, but maybe that is why I found a home in sports reporting and decided to stay there.

I suppose I could have gone and asked my bosses to send me to cover foreign wars or let me present the news but I never really wanted to rock the boat. I just wanted to be a journalist, I wanted to be at the heart of the story and I just loved the fact that the stories I ended up being at the heart of were about football.

There is a real sense of camaraderie in sports journalism and one thing you notice if you spend any time with football reporters is how well they all get along with each other. Of course, there is rivalry between them when it comes to breaking stories and landing big interviews but, by and large, they all seem to get on. If one of them breaks a big story then the rest of their colleagues will congratulate them on a job well done. You would think they would constantly be at each other's throats but from what I have seen the opposite is often the case.

Being a football reporter on a big national newspaper these days can be a real slog. There is, and always has been, the constant travel to games and press conferences, and nowadays lots of different platforms have to be provided with new content around the clock. These reporters frequently go to the same games and press conferences and although journalism can be a lonely job, a real camaraderie exists between them. They work as a team, especially when time is tight.

For instance, after a game they will split into groups and some will go to the managers' post-match press conferences while others will go to get quick interviews and quotes from the players. Once they have what they need, they share it between them on email as quickly as possible because they are frequently up against the clock. Evening games usually finish between 9.30 p.m. and 10 p.m. and deadlines to file stories and match reports are minutes away. You will not last long in that environment if you are selfish and only looking out for number one. Despite the fact that everyone writes their own pieces and has their own takes, whenever possible they all try to work together as a team and help each other out to make their lives and jobs just that little bit easier.

The same thing happens at pre-match news conferences, although the atmosphere is more relaxed because the pressure to hit a deadline is not so intense. Premier League managers have to speak to the media before and after every game and it is these encounters which generate many of the headlines and stories you read, listen to and watch. The newspaper reporters need a transcript of everything that is said and it would be pointless and time-consuming if they all sat around afterwards listening to their recordings of the press conference and each transcribing it word for word. What they do instead is divide the press conference into two- or three-minute chunks, and each one of them transcribes a different chunk. When they have done that, they share it among each other by email, which means they all have a full transcript of the press conference in a fraction of the time it would take if all of them were doing it on their own just for themselves.

Another interesting dynamic at these press conferences is how the journalists work together to get good stories from their exchanges with the managers or players. These press conferences typically last about twenty minutes. There are usually two sections and occasionally three. The first section is for the broadcast media and is filmed by TV cameras. This is when TV and radio reporters get to ask questions. Each reporter usually gets a maximum of three or four questions, although it used to be more.

The second section is for the written media and the cameras are usually turned off for this. It lasts about ten minutes and this is when newspaper reporters ask questions and the material is embargoed for use in the next day's newspapers. If the press conference is previewing a Sunday or Monday game, there will also be a short third section so reporters who are writing for the Sunday or Monday paper have fresh material.

The general public hardly ever get to see a press conference from start to finish because they are rarely filmed in full and you can only attend if you are an accredited journalist. If you did go to one, you would be struck by how the journalists often work together to extract the best possible material from the encounter. In the newspaper section, reporters only get one or two questions so they each try a different tack to probe and prod until they get something which hopefully will merit a big splash in their newspapers on the following day.

In the broadcast section of the press conference, a manager may have said he doesn't want to talk about a transfer target but he may be more relaxed in the newspaper section when the cameras are turned off and he is asked less direct questions. Whereas the TV and radio reporter may have to throw names of targets at the manager and ask questions about the big stories concerning that particular club, the newspaper reporter can afford to be more cute, considered or left-field in order to try and get the manager to open up. The newspaper reporters will be working together to get new material for themselves. They can't just ask the same questions and cover the same topics which were covered in the broadcast section because that material will be released instantly and will be all over the internet and social media straight away.

When it comes to building a real rapport with players and managers – and asking great questions – the best reporters are often those who work for the tabloids. Their knowledgeable and relaxed demeanour and their way with words often seem to put managers and players at ease. Consequently, that means they are much more likely to open up and say something interesting. I was at the back of a Chelsea press conference in 2017 when Antonio Conte was the head coach and Andrew Dillon of the *Sun* managed to get a great answer from him by asking a question which no one was expecting.

Dillon asked Conte what he was planning to do with his wife on Valentine's Day, which was just a few days away. Conte – and the whole room – laughed in surprise and we were laughing even more at the answer. Conte said he would be doing nothing with his wife because he would be watching Juventus play Porto on TV in the Champions League round of 16. Love would most certainly not be in the air for Mrs Conte.

That answer ended up being a page lead story in the *Sun* and it gave an interesting insight into just how obsessed Conte was with football. It also goes to show that in the newspaper section of press conferences, and when you get a chance in longer interviews, you don't always have to ask the obvious question. Sometimes, a more original and unexpected question can actually get you a more interesting and revealing answer.

Conte has always usually been good value when he talks to the press, so much so that an infamous outburst in a post-match press conference after his Tottenham side drew 3–3 at Southampton in March 2023 ended up costing him his job. At Chelsea, there always seemed to be something else going on behind the scenes at his press conferences, especially approaching the end of his final season in charge when he had fallen out with his employers over transfer strategy. There were also some memorable encounters when he was talking about his extremely strained relationship with combustible star striker Diego Costa.

At all those press conferences, there was a room full of journalists sitting in front of Conte trying to get him to open up as much as possible and they could only really do that by working together, by taking it in turns to ask questions to see how much they could get out of him. That is what happens at football press conferences almost every day of the season and that is how a lot of the stories you read, listen to and watch are generated. Despite popular misconceptions, a lot of the time, football reporters are working together – sometimes even unknowingly – to get the best possible quotes and stories.

These may seem like small, inconsequential details but when you are going to multiple games and press conferences every week for a whole season, and often during the summer as well, they can make a real difference as far as your workload is concerned. Of course, there are some reporters who don't get on with each other, but fallouts and confrontations happen a lot less than you might imagine. From what I have seen, there is teamwork and camaraderie on the pitch in football and in the press box as well. You may not like to hear it but my colleagues on newspapers, radio and TV are not the villains they are sometimes made out to be on social media. They are professionals who live and breathe the game, people who have had to work very hard to get to where they are, people who work very hard in often difficult circumstances under pressure in an industry that is highly competitive and constantly changing.

Although I have spent a lot of the past twenty years or so in TV and radio studios, I do try to get out and about to as many games and press conferences as possible, usually in my own time. I do it not because I get paid extra for it but because it helps me do a better job. You can't talk about teams, games or players with any real authority if you are just sitting at home watching on television. You can't talk about how players and managers think and feel if you don't go and speak to them and watch them live with your own eyes rather than through the filter of TV cameras.

Sometimes, a story is so big you just have to be at the centre of the action and that is exactly what happened in May 2013, when Sir Alex Ferguson announced that he was retiring as Manchester United manager after twenty-six years in charge. Football stories don't get much bigger, so I got up to United's Carrington training ground as quickly as possible to join all the other reporters and TV crews from around the world who were covering the story. As I was standing there, in between live TV broadcasts every hour, I was thinking about how I could move the story on. How could I get some fresh material before anybody else? I had known Sir Alex for a long time and I considered myself to be pretty close to him – as close as a journalist could get. It was a very significant and emotional day for him and I didn't fancy my chances of success when I tried to get in touch. Luckily, I had more luck with United's first-team coach, René Meulensteen.

I asked if there was any chance of a quick interview. René was inside the training ground taking in the events of that momentous day. He messaged back to say he would be leaving in about five minutes and he would stop and roll down his car window and speak to me on his way out. Sure enough, a few minutes later, René turned up, rolled down his window and spoke to me about what had just been happening inside Carrington, what the mood was and how Sir Alex had gone about breaking the news to everyone. Of course, I was more than happy to share the quotes from the interview with all the other reporters and broadcasters there and it was just another example of how we all work together on all manner of stories, no matter how big or small.

Whatever kind of story you are working on, you always have to push yourself, be creative and try to come up with a new angle. I was working at STV when Brian Laudrup was making a real impact at Rangers after they signed him for £2.3 million from Fiorentina in the summer of 1994. I told my bosses that no one knew Laudrup better than his brother Michael, who was playing for Real Madrid at the time, and they agreed to let me go to Spain to speak to him. Then it dawned on me that I had to somehow get in touch with Michael and convince him to talk to me. Luckily, I managed to do that with the minimum of fuss because Michael is such a gentleman and he agreed to do the interview even though we had never met before. I flew out to Spain with a cameraman and we came back a day later with a great interview. Funnily enough, I met Michael again about twenty years later when he was managing Swansea City and he still remembered meeting me to talk about his kid brother.

The fundamentals of journalism don't change just because you are reporting on something as relatively unimportant, in the grand scheme of things, as football or transfers. You still have to have that hunger and drive to gather news, to find out things that some people may not want you to know. Living in the social media age means you are going to get criticised, people are going to accuse you of not knowing what you are talking about, people are going to accuse you of lying or spreading fake news. You have to block all that negativity out and trust yourself and stick to the basics of journalism. Check everything and make sure every word you write or say counts and is fair and accurate. And once in a while, try and think outside the box.

That's what I did before a crucial Euro 2000 play-off first leg game between Scotland and England at Hampden Park in November 1999. I wanted to get something different, something no one else had, and that is why I ended up sitting in front of the Chancellor of the Exchequer at the time – and future Prime Minister – Gordon Brown. I had got to know Gordon a little bit when he used to pop into STV's offices, and I seem to remember he even tried his hand at TV presenting for a while. Anyway, it was well known that he liked his football and he was very gracious during our interview as I asked him what it would feel like to beat Prime Minister Tony Blair's England and, as a numbers man, what formation he would recommend: 4–4–2 or 5–4–1? Of course, in the end that was all academic because England won 2–0 in Glasgow thanks to two Paul Scholes goals. Scotland put up a brave fight in the second leg at Wembley but they could only win 1–0 and that meant that it was England who ended up qualifying for the Euros.

I have lots of contacts now and I have so far managed to get my fair share of big interviews, but I don't want to make it sound like my career has been plain sailing. It certainly hasn't been a succession of big transfer stories and headline interviews. Far from it, every career has its share of highs and lows, especially in an industry as competitive, fast-moving and fast-changing as journalism.

The important thing is to keep things in perspective and never stop believing in yourself and your ability to do the job effectively. You can't do that by sitting at home or sitting in the office feeling sorry for yourself. You have to get out there and find stories and contacts and people who will talk to you. Rejection is part and parcel of the game no matter who you are. You just have to get over it as quickly as possible. It is just another hurdle you have to overcome. Never accept rejection. Rejection is usually just one person's point of view. If your face doesn't fit in one place, it will fit somewhere else. Never forget that.

Rejection and criticism are just things you have to learn to deal with, no matter who you are, no matter what part of the football business you work in and no matter how successful you may think you are. In April 2023, I went to watch Aston Villa beat Newcastle United 3–0 at Villa Park. I go to lots of games on my days off and I don't just go to watch football. I go to interview players and managers, which I record on my phone, and I go to make contacts and also to speak to fans and gauge their mood.

I was leaving Villa Park after interviewing John McGinn in the players' tunnel and I was heading out towards the train station when I saw Tyrone Mings in the car park talking to a group of people. I went over to speak to him but it would be fair to say that the Villa centre-back wasn't particularly overjoyed to see me. It soon became apparent that he wasn't happy with some of the things that had been said about him on my radio show, particularly by my colleague Simon Jordan. At the time, Mings was proving a lot of people wrong with his performances at the heart of the Villa defence and I told him to keep doing what he was doing.

That is what you have to do if you are a player and that is what you have to do if you are a journalist or anybody else in any walk of life. If people doubt or criticise you, if they ridicule or belittle you, if they mock or bully you, you have to prove them wrong. Block out the noise, ignore the hate, don't let people who don't know you define you. You don't lie, you don't make it up and you don't spread fake news. Journalism is a tough business. Master the basics, don't stop working and don't stop believing in yourself.

Chapter 5

Let's Spend the Night Together

Some people think football reporters love transfer deadline day and they blame us for what it has become. Step back though and ask yourself a simple question – would clubs stop spending crazy amounts of money on players if there were no journalists to report on the deals?

Football reporters all grew up loving the game, they worked hard to get to where they are and when they started out they weren't dreaming of reporting on the twists and turns of transfer sagas. They wanted to write and talk about the game and the players, the drama and the excitement, they didn't dream about writing one day that Manchester United were one of the clubs preparing to launch a bid to sign Moisés Caicedo.

There's a generation of supporters now who seem to be more interested in transfers than the actual football. The level of interest all around the world is phenomenal. You could argue now that if you gave the fan of one of the so-called big clubs a choice between winning the FA Cup or signing one of the world's best players, most would go for the second option.

Of course, if you are obsessed with transfers then the two deadline days every year are unmissable occasions. For reporters, they are two of the longest days of the year, but in a funny way they can be easier and more enjoyable than the rest of the window. On the final day, time is running out and the people involved in deals are desperate to make them happen, so you tend to get more information from them throughout the day. They don't have to keep everything secret any more and it sometimes feels like they want to be part of the drama as well. Contacts who have given very little away for weeks suddenly start giving you the inside track on what is going on behind the scenes. And the closer you get to the deadline, the more people open up.

One of the big dramas on deadline day in January 2023 was a deal that didn't happen. It all unravelled in the final hour of the window and luckily I had good contacts at both ends of the deal who kept me right across what was happening in real time.

The story really started in 2020 when Chelsea signed Hakim Ziyech from Ajax for €40 million. Ziyech was a brilliant wide player with a fantastic left foot, but his performances at Chelsea were inconsistent and he fell out of favour under Thomas Tuchel, who replaced Frank Lampard as manager in January 2021.

Away from his club, Ziyech was one of the stars of the 2022 World Cup as his Morocco team made it to the semi-finals. Wherever I went in Qatar I would be stopped by

Moroccans and asked why Ziyech was not playing regularly for Chelsea. It was obvious that Ziyech needed to change clubs and he seemed to have got his dream move just weeks after the World Cup when Paris Saint-Germain tried to sign him on deadline day in January 2023.

The proposed move ended up being 'an absolute shambles' according to senior figures at the French club, so much so that sources at the club said they decided never to do business with Chelsea again. Ziyech, for his part, was distraught when the move failed to materialise, especially because he did everything he could to make it happen.

Playing for a French club as big as PSG is a dream for any Moroccan player because of the Moroccan diaspora in France. Ziyech was so desperate for the move he was reportedly willing to pay out of his own pocket to make it happen, even though it appeared that he might find it even more difficult to start games at PSG than he had at Chelsea. After all, at the time, PSG already had an incredible front three of Lionel Messi, Kylian Mbappé and Neymar.

Ziyech didn't care about the competition for places provided by that superstar trio. He was up for the challenge and playing with players of that calibre was one of the attractions of moving to Paris. That's why, as the clock ticked away on deadline day, he was in PSG's offices in the French capital, having already passed his medical. He was ready to complete the deal and all that needed to be done was for Chelsea to sign the loan agreement and email it back to PSG. As the hours started drifting by, Ziyech and his agent started getting anxious because it looked like Chelsea were dragging their feet. Ziyech took matters into his own hands and personally messaged the club's co-owner, Todd Boehly, begging him to speed things up so he could get his dream move.

To say PSG were disappointed with the way things turned out on the night of Tuesday 31 January 2023 would be an understatement. As far as they were concerned, they had emailed all the relevant paperwork to Chelsea at 9.40 p.m. – one hour and twenty minutes before the 11 p.m. deadline. That should have been plenty of time for Chelsea to sign the loan agreement and email it back, but after waiting for an hour, PSG officials, Ziyech and his agent were getting worried. They called Chelsea four times, at 10.46 p.m., 10.48 p.m., 10.49 p.m. and 10.50 p.m., but no one answered. Finally, at 10.55 p.m., just five minutes before the deadline, PSG received an email back from Chelsea, but when they opened the attachment it was the wrong document and even that was not signed.

PSG refused to give up and at 10.56 p.m. they emailed the loan agreement to Chelsea again, signed by them and Ziyech. Then they waited. All hope was not lost because there were still four minutes to the deadline. At 10.58 p.m., Chelsea replied that they had already sent the signed agreement back, but the version attached was the wrong document again and it was still not signed. Finally, at 11.03 p.m. PSG received the correct signed document back and they uploaded it onto the Ligue de Football website (LFP) a minute later.

They had missed the deadline by four minutes. After losing their appeal to the LFP legal committee the following day, PSG and Ziyech had to accept the deal was off. The player was bitterly disappointed but he returned to London and started for Chelsea three days later in the goalless draw with Fulham at Stamford Bridge. Some players would have thrown their toys out of their pram; some players would have gone on strike. You have to say Ziyech showed great professionalism by knuckling down and getting back to work straight away.

Although PSG had to accept the transfer was off, behind the scenes they were fuming and they vowed not to forgive or forget. 'Chelsea will not darken PSG's doorstep again,' a source in Paris said. 'It was an absolute shambles. This is not how you do business or treat a player. At lunchtime on Tuesday, the player arrived in Paris with all the procedures set up for a loan deal, with just a final discussion on the option to buy or not and the fee to be agreed.'

According to sources at the club, 'Ziyech was at PSG's offices from early evening onwards when he and his agent started to get concerned, but there was no indication that the deal wouldn't happen. The player started texting Boehly directly, pleading to hurry up. He was even contributing personally towards the financials to get the deal done.'

Of course, the deal wasn't done and there wasn't anything PSG could do about it. In any case, there are two sides to every story and although Chelsea did not want to comment about what had happened, they blamed a technical issue for the deal collapsing at the eleventh hour. People may also blame PSG and say it was their fault for leaving it so late to get the deal done. If they really wanted the player, why did they wait until the final day of the window to make their move? In PSG's defence, it has to be said that negotiations during windows are like a high-stakes game of poker – you often have to wait until the last possible minute to get the best deal and leaving it so late obviously means there is a risk of the deal not happening at all. And it is not all just about brinkmanship either, because a lot of deals depend on other deals. For instance, a club might not want to buy a striker until they've sold a striker or a club might not want to sell a midfielder until they have signed a midfielder. By the way, in case you are wondering, Ziyech did finally get his move away from Chelsea but he had to wait until August 2023 when he joined Galatasaray on loan with an option to buy.

One of the most famous, or should I say infamous, transfer deadline day dramas was about a deal that didn't end up happening on 31 January 2013. The man at the centre of all the drama was Peter Odemwingie, who was playing for West Bromwich Albion in the Premier League at the time. I have got to know Odemwingie over the years and it is testament to his strength of character and resilience that he is so honest and open about what went wrong for him that winter's night in west London. Other players might be too embarrassed or ashamed to talk about what happened but Odemwingie believes the best way to deal with any issue is to confront it head on. He doesn't like running away from anything, even if it was something which really threatened to damage his reputation and standing in the game.

During the window in question, it was well known that Odemwingie would welcome a move away from West Brom and he had offers to move to clubs in Dubai and Qatar. He kept his options open until the morning of deadline day, when he was presented with a proposal by West Brom which would see him move to London to play for Queens Park Rangers. They were also in the Premier League at the time but they were bottom of the table and Harry Redknapp had replaced Mark Hughes as manager five weeks before the window opened.

A deal had been agreed in principle which valued Odemwingie at £3.5 million rising to £4.2 million. West Brom told him that, despite time running out, the opportunity was there for the transfer to happen. Odemwingie was keen on the move and on deadline day you have to be in the right place at the right time to get a deal done. With that in mind and with the clock ticking, he headed down to London. That's when things started to go wrong. As he got closer and closer to the capital he became more and more suspicious that something was not quite right. His messages and calls were not being answered, whereas if everything had been going according to plan people would have been jumping through hoops to track his progress to make sure he got to QPR in time to complete the deal.

There were fans and TV cameras waiting outside when Odemwingie got to Loftus Road at about 7 p.m. It was a busy day at the club because they were five points adrift at the bottom of the Premier League and Redknapp and club executives were hard at work trying to tie up deals for other players like Jermaine Jenas, Christopher Samba and Andros Townsend.

Out of common courtesy, Odemwingie wound down his window, signed autographs and answered a few questions from a reporter. As he was speaking, it dawned on him that being interviewed outside Loftus Road when he was still a West Brom player could make it look like he was trying to push through a move to QPR. That is not what he was trying to do and deep down he knew there were serious problems with the deal. Those serious problems turned out to be the fact that his deal depended on Junior Hoilett moving in the opposite direction from QPR to West Brom.

'It was a complete mess,' Odemwingie said, 'involving agents, imaginary agents and intermediaries. People got involved in the deal and they were trying to get themselves a payday. Junior Hoilett appeared to be part of the deal but I had no knowledge of that.

'The deal never materialised and I never even got close to a medical. What annoys me is that there were individuals who were involved in what happened that day who still won't account for their actions. They all want to protect their reputation at the expense of mine. I've had zero apologies from anyone about what happened.

'Anyway, I bounced back at Stoke City and they took me without any judgement. I played with a smile on my face again there and I played well and I scored goals. People still talk to me about what happened that night at QPR but I have moved on. Who knows, maybe one day I will name names.'

Odemwingie deserves to be remembered for much more than an embarrassing night in west London. He was a very good player who represented Nigeria sixty-three times and he has always been a real gentleman. He is also in good company when it comes to players who were at the centre of deadline dramas.

If you leave it late, there's always a chance that things are going to go wrong. That's what happened with John Hartson in August 2000, although the deadline he was trying to beat was the one imposed by UEFA for players to be registered to play in the Champions League. Hartson was twenty-five at the time and he was racing against the clock to swap relegated Wimbledon for Rangers, who were the champions of Scotland. If everything went according to plan he would be waving goodbye to the second tier of English football to play against some of the best players in the world in the Champions League.

Hartson was on international duty when the Wales manager, Mark Hughes, told him they had just received a fax at the team hotel which said Rangers had made a £6 million bid to sign him. Things had to move fast and Rangers had sent a plane to pick up the player and his father from Cardiff airport and fly them to Glasgow to have his medical and complete the deal.

Hartson was overjoyed about the prospect of playing for

Rangers, but as he flew north he was also concerned because he knew he had already failed medicals at Tottenham Hotspur and Charlton Athletic, and he was worried that history was going to repeat itself.

When he arrived in Glasgow he headed straight to Ibrox and he remembers walking along the side of the pitch and seeing Dutch midfielder Ronald de Boer in the centre circle. 'I shouted to him that I would be out on the pitch taking pictures with him soon,' Hartson said. 'I was trying to put my doubts about the medical to the back of my mind.'

Hartson went to hospital to have his medical, including knee scans, and then he returned to Ibrox to discuss the terms of his five-year contract with chairman David Murray and manager Dick Advocaat. It was during those talks that his worst fears were realised when a member of Rangers' medical team arrived to break the news that they could not proceed with the deal because of the results of the medical. Hartson was gutted but there was nothing anyone could do. Everyone said sorry to him and he headed back to Cardiff to join up again with the Wales squad and deal with the disappointment of a third move falling through because of a failed medical.

While Rangers started their Scottish Premier League and Champions League campaign, Hartson kicked off the new season playing for Wimbledon in the First Division. He stayed at Wimbledon until he returned to the Premier League after signing a pay-as-you-play deal with Coventry City in February 2001. He only played for Coventry twelve times because, just six months after he arrived there, he got a call from Celtic manager Martin O'Neill.

'He basically said he wanted to take a punt on me,' Hartson said. 'I didn't have a medical because if I'd had one I would probably have failed it. The same problem would have shown up even though I was fit to play. I think Celtic ended up paying £6 million for me. I was high as a kite when I signed that four-year contract. I ended up staying for five years.

'I scored 110 goals for Celtic and nine of them were against Rangers. During the whole time I was there I didn't have a single problem with my knee and I never missed a single training session because of it. Missing out on the move to Rangers and then signing for Celtic was a real sliding doors moment for me.'

Hartson is also too modest to mention that he won six major trophies in his time at Celtic including three Scottish Premier League titles. I actually still remember the day he became a Celtic player. The club had signed Hartson, Steve Guppy and Momo Sylla on the same day and I knew that Hartson was staying at One Devonshire Gardens Hotel in Glasgow. I went there to see if I could get an interview with him before he was introduced to the media at the official Celtic press conference. I waited outside the hotel until Hartson and Guppy came out and I asked them for a quick word. Guppy wasn't keen because he thought they would get in trouble with Celtic but that didn't seem to bother Hartson too much. 'No problem, Jim,' he said. 'Let's do it.'

Over the years I have done a lot of transfer interviews and one of my favourite people to speak to has been my good friend Harry Redknapp, who was of course involved in Peter Odemwingie's on–off move to QPR. Transfer deadline days don't quite feel the same since Harry retired as a manager. I think he became synonymous with the day not because he was always doing last-minute deals, but because he was always willing to help out journalists and be as honest and open as he could be with his club's fans. Like all managerial careers, Harry had his fair share of highs and lows but the highs far outweighed the lows. After all, this was a man who won the FA Cup with Portsmouth and took Tottenham from the bottom of the Premier League to the Champions League a few years later.

I was speaking to Harry recently after he had just finished a round of golf at Loch Lomond and we were reminiscing about deadline days. He had so many memories of them and what really stood out for him was the theatre and the suspense – he loved being part of all the drama when he was a manager. Sometimes it was hectic and dramatic but that's why he loved it, even though with the clock ticking things could always go wrong at the last minute. Looking back now over all those years, he can see the funny side of some of the deals that went wrong.

One that really sticks in Harry's mind is Tottenham failing to sign Blackpool midfielder Charlie Adam by a matter of minutes on deadline day in January 2011. Liverpool had been in talks to sign Adam and when they failed to agree a fee with Blackpool, Tottenham made their move on deadline day. The only problem was that they had trouble getting hold of the player to get the deal done and once they found him there were more issues finding the Blackpool officials who needed to sign the paperwork. Adam did eventually move on from Blackpool in the summer after they were relegated – but unfortunately for Harry it was to Liverpool.

If Spurs had managed to sign Adam he would have ended up playing in the same side as Rafael van der Vaart, a player Harry thinks is his best deadline day buy. Harry was only told he was in with a chance of signing Van der Vaart two hours before the window was set to close at 6 p.m. on Tuesday 31 August 2010. He had assumed Van der Vaart was moving from Real Madrid to Bayern Munich, until he got a phone call at 4 p.m. saying there was a deal to be done for £8 million if Spurs could move quickly. That's exactly what they did but, because of unfortunate technical problems with computers, the paperwork which needed to be signed off by Real Madrid and Spurs wasn't completed in time. Spurs and Harry didn't give up though. They appealed for special dispensation from the Premier League and, after an anxious wait, the approval came through the following day.

There was a real sense of excitement at White Hart Lane about Spurs signing a world-class player like Van der Vaart from a club like Real Madrid. At twenty-seven, he was in the prime of his career and he had already played eighty-three times for the Netherlands. He quickly established himself as a firm fans' favourite, playing alongside players like Luka Modric and Gareth Bale. Spurs fans still have great memories of his performances and goals in two wins against Arsenal in 2010 and 2011.

Although it looked like Van der Vaart was going to have a long and successful career at Spurs, things changed when André Villas-Boas replaced Harry as Tottenham manager in the summer of 2012. Van der Vaart didn't appear to be in the new manager's long-term plans and he was allowed to return to Hamburg in a £10 million deal. He left the Tottenham fans with some great memories and they still show their appreciation by chanting his name to the tune of 'Baby Give It Up' by KC and The Sunshine Band.

Of course, Harry wasn't just famous for pulling off some great deals on deadline day, he was also famous for speaking to reporters through the window of his Range Rover. It almost became a ritual on deadline day for Harry to wind his window down and give the poor reporters who had been waiting outside the training ground all day – in the freezing cold if it was the January window – a few words about the state of play at the club on one of the most important days of the football calendar.

Why did Harry always stop and talk when most other managers would drive straight by? I think part of the reason is that Harry is someone who is from a generation when players and managers mixed much more easily with journalists. They all tended to come from similar backgrounds and live similar kinds of lives, and they all got on and respected each other most of the time. Another reason why

Harry always stopped is that he really is a genuinely nice guy and it wouldn't even cross his mind to blank anybody, especially someone who had been waiting outdoors for hours to speak to him.

I also think that Harry loved deadline day and loved being part of it. He knew that the fans of his club wanted the very latest information and the best way for him to provide that was to speak to the media. He had a genuine connection with journalists and he would think nothing of inviting them into the training ground if it was a particularly cold day and giving them a cup of tea, a bacon roll and what they really wanted – the latest information on the deals he was working on.

I am still in regular touch with Harry and, even though he has retired from management, I still try and get him involved on deadline days on my radio shows. My routine at talk-SPORT on deadline days is different to the days when I was working on TV because I am on air much earlier. In my TV days I was always on in the evenings in the last few hours of the window, but I am on the radio in the mornings and in the evenings at talkSPORT, so deadline days have now turned into all-day marathons for me.

I always set the alarm for 6.30 a.m. on the big day and I am out of my door forty-five minutes later for the fifteen-minute walk to the studio. My routine is the same as any other weekday. I stop to buy coffee for me and my producers and, while I am waiting, I will be checking my phone for messages from contacts who are up as early as me. I often get recognised on my way to work and especially on deadline day. People want to stop and talk about transfers and I am more than happy to tell them what I know.

The January 2023 window was the busiest Premier League winter window ever and that meant most days I was being stopped by people who wanted to know what was happening with Enzo Fernández or Moisés Caicedo or Mykhailo Mudryk.

Fernández and Caicedo were two of the big stories of the month and luckily I had good contacts around both of the potential deals. People close to Caicedo were hoping that he would move to Arsenal right up until deadline day, but I was told consistently that Brighton would not let him go. I checked a couple of times on deadline day and the message I got back was loud and clear: 'Jim, the player will not be moving. I mean what I say.' That was good enough for me. Others may have been reporting that there was still a chance the player would move, that Arsenal might make another late bid, but I knew the person I was dealing with was senior enough to know what was going on and there was no reason for him to mislead me.

I have to admit I got just a little bit concerned when another journalist called me and told me to watch out for an £80 million bid from Arsenal but I held firm, I backed myself and I trusted my source.

Caicedo ended up staying at Brighton – until he moved to Chelsea in August 2023 – and I called my source the next day to thank him for all his help and guidance during the window. Having good contacts is one of the most important things if you want to break stories on deadline days. You have to be confident if you want to be a reporter and you have to be a people person. Nobody is going to open up to you or trust you if they don't like you or if they don't like your company.

Don't get me wrong, I don't spend my life hanging out with players and billionaire owners, but it is part of my job to get to know as many of them as possible, to build up a professional relationship with them. Sometimes they do become friends and if that happens, that's great but that's not my motivation for doing this job; my motivation is my love of the game and my love of journalism.

Luckily, I also had a good contact for the really big story of deadline day, Enzo Fernández moving from Benfica to Chelsea in a British record £107 million transfer. My best contact on this deal was about as good a contact as you can get. I was slightly taken aback because the first time I met him, he asked for my number and not the other way round, which is usually what happens.

Anyway, this contact had kept me right across the Fernández deal throughout January. It was a real saga because Benfica didn't want to sell but the player wanted to move and Chelsea were desperate to do the deal. My contact had said all along that the deal could go right to the wire and that is exactly what happened. And when I say right to the wire, I mean right to the wire.

It was only at 10 p.m., with just an hour to go until the

window closed, that I got the green light to report that Fernández was going to be a Chelsea player. Having said that, there was still a chance the deal would not go through because there was so little time left to complete the paperwork.

With just five minutes to go until the 11 p.m. deadline, I was still in the dark about whether the deal was going to happen until I got a very short message which I read out live on air: 'We've got extra sixty minutes.' Chelsea had been given more time to get the deal done but it was still touch and go whether it was going to happen. The major players in the deal were all over the world – one of them was in Los Angeles, one in London and one in Lisbon.

The deal did finally get done just before midnight and I only found out the next day that it was just three minutes away from not happening at all. At 11.57 p.m. Chelsea officials were frantically FaceTiming Fernández in Lisbon to talk him through how to sign the paperwork remotely on his laptop.

I was shattered and elated as I walked home at 1 a.m. I had to be awake at 6.30 a.m. to go back to work but I love my job and I wouldn't change it for anything.

I pretty much enjoy everything about deadline day except maybe some of the criticism you get from people who look down their noses at it and dismiss it all as gossip and a big circus. Guess what? If you don't like it, you don't have to watch it or listen to it or read about it. There are lots of other things you can do with your time. For instance, I'm not a big fan of the Eurovision Song Contest but I don't want it banned and I don't complain about it because millions of people around the world love and enjoy it.

Anyone who criticises the journalists who report on transfers should look at the end results. Only very rarely does what we say not happen and when it doesn't happen, we don't hide. We try and find out why it didn't happen and we explain what we have found out. The best transfer reporters are trained journalists with years of experience and hundreds, if not thousands, of contacts on their phones. They work hard and they hold their hands up when they get something wrong. Credibility is everything, especially on deadline days when millions are watching and listening to everything you say.

Of course, if you are one of the best players in the world you can create your own deadline day and that is exactly what Harry Kane did in the summer of 2023. Although the official deadline day for that window was 1 September, Kane wanted his future sorted out well before then. The England captain wanted to know one way or the other who he would be playing for when the season started – Tottenham or Bayern Munich?

As far as he was concerned, his deadline day was Friday 11 August and there were some very good reasons for that. Tottenham's first Premier League game of the season was on Sunday 13 August and Kane felt it would be disrespectful to Tottenham supporters, head coach Ange Postecoglou and his teammates if he was to start the season playing for Spurs and then leave for Bayern a few days or weeks later. Kane also had personal, family reasons for not wanting the potential move to drag on all summer. His wife was pregnant and due to give birth soon and he needed to know where he would be living and working as soon as possible.

Bayern also wanted a deal to be done on that Friday so they could register Kane by 3 p.m. to ensure that he could play in the German Super Cup final the following day.

Kane's very own deadline day turned out to be just as dramatic as a real one. He was being driven to Stansted airport at 7 a.m. for a private jet flight to Munich when he was told the deal had not been totally agreed between all parties yet, and he should stay in the UK until Bayern gave him the all-clear to fly.

Negotiations between Bayern and Tottenham had not been straightforward. Bayern's opening offer in June had been worth only £60 million plus add ons for a player Tottenham valued at more than £100 million, even though he had only a year left on his contract. After more bids and talks, there was finally a breakthrough on Thursday 10 August with the two clubs agreeing a deal worth an initial £86 million. Kane decided to accept Bayern's offer later the same day and the stage was set for him to fly to Munich early on Friday morning.

That was the plan but on Friday morning he was sitting and waiting at a family home near Stansted when he should have been high above the clouds flying to Munich to beat the 3 p.m. deadline to register in time for Saturday night's final.

As far as Tottenham were concerned, Kane was free to fly and they had given him permission to travel to Munich to complete the formalities of the transfer. But Bayern were not prepared to let him arrive in Germany until they were satisfied everything had been agreed and there was no way Kane was going to take any risks until the remaining issues between the parties had been resolved.

Kane waited and waited until just before 3 p.m. when he was given the all-clear to fly by Bayern. Within minutes he was back on the road on the way to Stansted and after being stuck in traffic he finally took off for Munich close to 5 p.m., some nine hours later than planned.

It was better late than never for Bayern and after a dogged pursuit and a club-record transfer fee they signed a worthy successor to Robert Lewandowski. They had also managed to convince the German league to extend the registration deadline by twenty-four hours to 3 p.m. on Saturday so Kane could play in the Super Cup final.

Kane came on as a second-half substitute but unfortunately a rollercoaster few days ended with a 3–0 defeat by RB Leipzig. Playing for a club as big as Bayern though means Kane can look forward to lots more finals and plenty of trophies.

He deserves a lot of credit for accepting the challenge to play in Germany even though his departure is a great loss for English football – unless you are an Arsenal fan.

Chapter 6

What Do You Think they're Smoking Over there at Emirates?

Some things are just not meant to be. Every life is a series of missed opportunities. You see something you want, you don't get it and you spend the rest of your days wondering what your life would have been like if you had got what you had wanted. Or you wonder what life would have been like if you hadn't let something go; if you had fought harder to keep it or if you had just made a different decision.

It's easy to be too hard on yourself in life and it's easy to be too hard on yourself in the transfer market. It is a market, after all, so it's only natural that people will buy and sell things they later regret having bought and sold. Or they will regret not buying when they had the chance. Although regrets are something you have to deal with in life, they can be much more difficult to handle in football. As a manager, you will have to spend almost every day of your life for years with that striker you spent millions on who never scores. Or you will have to watch the striker you sold or missed out on scoring for someone else every week.

The only consolation for managers is that when things go wrong, the money they've wasted is not their own, otherwise it would hurt even more. Making mistakes can have serious consequences though, and the bigger the mistake the more likely it is to lead to a manager losing his job.

Getting sacked as a manager is an occupational hazard and so is buying the wrong player. It would be easy to spend a whole chapter of this book listing all the deals that turned out to be total failures but that wouldn't be fair on the players or their managers and there are already lots of lists like that on the internet. Every deal looks good on paper, otherwise the club wouldn't have signed the player in the first place, and transfers don't work out for numerous reasons. It's not always just because the player is not any good. Players may find it too difficult to settle at their new club, their family may be unhappy moving or living in a different country, the style of play at a new club may not suit the player, a new manager might come in who doesn't rate him, he could have personal problems nobody knows about.

We shouldn't jump on a player's back when a deal doesn't work out. We can all reel off a long list of big-money deals that have turned out to be disasters but, at the end of the day, we don't know all the facts, we don't know what is going on behind the scenes. Hand on heart, can you honestly say that everything you have bought in your life has turned out to be value-for-money and a great deal? That's why, whenever I'm reporting on a transfer, I try to make sure there's a little voice in the back of my head telling me, 'Don't get carried away. There's probably a 50 per cent chance this deal is not going to work out.'

I'm not sure that voice was there on Monday 31 January 2011 when Chelsea signed Fernando Torres from Liverpool for £50 million, which was a British record at the time. That deadline day was one of the most dramatic I can remember, because Liverpool also bought Luis Suárez from Ajax and Andy Carroll from Newcastle United, and Chelsea signed David Luiz from Benfica as well. I can remember talking over live pictures of a car with blacked-out windows arriving at Chelsea's training ground in Cobham, Surrey. I couldn't be sure, but all the information I was getting was that it was Torres in the car, he really was moving and, while Chelsea fans were celebrating an incredible transfer coup, Liverpool supporters were wondering what the hell was going on.

Rafa Benítez had spent £24 million on Torres in 2007 to help turn Liverpool from one of Europe's best cup sides into regular Premier League title challengers. In his second season, Liverpool went close to bringing the title back to Anfield. They lost just twice in the league all season and they beat Manchester United home and away, but they still finished four points behind Sir Alex Ferguson's champions.

Chelsea — and especially owner Roman Abramovich — had wanted Torres for a long time and even though they already had Didier Drogba and Nicolas Anelka up front, they made a big move for the Spain striker in the 2011 winter window. Torres was one of Abramovich's favourite players and in those days the Russian billionaire invariably got what he wanted. Abramovich was determined to get Torres and he was going to stop at nothing to get his man. Signing Torres also had the added benefit, as far as Chelsea were concerned, of depriving one of their rivals of all his goals.

Liverpool were unhappy with all the noise surrounding Torres during that window and they were dismayed when he handed in a transfer request three days before deadline day. Torres was rumoured to have a £50 million release clause in his contract which could be activated if Liverpool failed to qualify for the Champions League. They finally decided to let him go that January when they were seventh in the Premier League.

Torres scored twice in his penultimate game for Liverpool, away at Wolves on 22 January 2011, which is one more than he scored for Chelsea during the rest of that season after his record-breaking deadline day move. It took Torres almost three months, fourteen appearances and 903 minutes to score his first Chelsea goal – and things didn't get much better for him after that left-foot strike against West Ham United in a 3–0 win at Stamford Bridge. Chelsea, who had won the title the season before Torres arrived, finished second in the table behind Manchester United.

Torres wasn't in Chelsea's starting line-up for the Champions League final against Bayern Munich at the end of the following season. Chelsea manager Roberto Di Matteo started with Drogba up front on his own, and Torres replaced Salomon Kalou in the eighty-fourth minute, seconds after Thomas Müller had put Bayern in front. Drogba equalised with just two minutes of normal time left and he also scored the decisive final penalty in the shootout. Torres wasn't one of the five designated penalty takers and, although he helped Chelsea win the Champions League, he never won the title at Stamford Bridge, or at any of his other clubs, but he did win the World Cup and two European Championships with Spain.

It would be easy to call Torres a flop at Chelsea, especially because he scored only twenty league goals over four seasons before he joined AC Milan on loan in 2014, but there were many reasons why the move didn't work out and no one would say it was because he is not a very good player. A combination of injuries and loss of form undermined his confidence, and they were the reasons behind his disappointing spell at Chelsea. Few people could have predicted that he would struggle so much at Stamford Bridge after scoring eighty-one times for Liverpool in three and a half seasons. Don't forget he had also won the World Cup in 2010 – even though he didn't score in South Africa as Spain lifted the trophy after scoring a record low eight goals in the whole tournament.

Torres is a very understated, humble individual and the last time I met him was after he scored with a free header for Atlético Madrid in a friendly 3–2 win against Brighton in August 2017. It was a beautiful summer's day on the south coast and Torres was pleased to be back in England. I remember that day well because it was one of the few occasions when I have met the legendary Atlético manager and former Argentina midfielder Diego Simeone. I didn't know quite what to expect, because Simeone had a fearsome reputation as a player and he has not mellowed out much since he became a manager in 2006. I needn't have worried because he turned out to be an absolute gentleman, maybe because Atlético had won – or maybe because it had only been a friendly.

I would love to see him manage in England one day and I know a couple of agents have tried to get him a job at two big clubs in the Premier League. It would be fascinating to see him at a club like Chelsea, where he has been linked with the manager's job for a long time. He would have more money to spend on players there than he has been used to at Atlético and it would be interesting to see if he could improve the players already at the club and also sign players who can handle the pressure and expectations of playing for Chelsea. Too many players have failed to make an impact after big-money moves to Chelsea and it was an issue at the club long before the club's American owners arrived in London in 2022.

People have been making mistakes and making the wrong calls about buying and selling players since before the transfer window even existed. It's not just your average managers who get things wrong: even the very best in the business have made very big and sometimes very expensive mistakes. Take Sir Alex Ferguson. He is the greatest manager ever

– sorry, Pep – but his record wasn't perfect when it comes to transfers. No one's ever is.

Ferguson didn't make too many mistakes, but one he did appear to make – in hindsight – was deciding in 1989 that Paul McGrath's knee injuries and off-field problems meant he was surplus to requirements at Old Trafford. McGrath went on to prove he was one of the best defenders in the world during eight seasons at Aston Villa. He was also outstanding for Ireland at the 1990 and 1994 World Cups. Plenty of people who saw him play would say that, at his peak, he was one of the greatest defenders of all time, right up there with Franco Baresi, Franz Beckenbauer, Bobby Moore and Paolo Maldini. Along with the likes of Roy Keane and Liam Brady, he is one of Ireland's all-time great players. His talent and ability deserved more than an FA Cup, two League Cups and the 1992–93 PFA Player of the Year award.

There is another side to the story though. Perhaps, if you look at the bigger picture, Ferguson was right to let McGrath go. Perhaps he needed to make big changes, big calls to make United winners again and that is exactly what he did. That's not to take anything away from McGrath either. Sometimes players need a move to reignite their careers and sometimes clubs need to move on players for reasons which are not always apparent.

McGrath is a gentle giant and an absolutely charming character. I have met him a few times and spoken to many of his former teammates who still talk in glowing terms about just how good a player he was. He has also written a raw and harrowing autobiography, *Back From The Brink*, which describes in unflinching detail his struggles with alcoholism and what it has done to him and his friends and family. It is a testament to his character that he has faced up to his demons and beaten them.

McGrath knew the writing was on the wall for him in Manchester from Ferguson's very first game as United manager, when he was played out of position in midfield and substituted in the second half away at Oxford United in November 1986. United lost that game 2–0 and there were plenty of lows and lots of changes to personnel before Ferguson made United league champions again for the first time in twenty-six years in 1993. Looking back now, McGrath can see the bigger picture and he is the first to admit that Ferguson made the right call by letting him know that he didn't have a future at Old Trafford.

There were no transfer windows in those days and Ferguson did some of his best business before they were introduced in the Premier League for the 2002–03 season. In January 1995, Ferguson shocked the football world by convincing Kevin Keegan to sell him Newcastle United striker Andy Cole in a £7 million deal. Cole had scored sixty-eight times in three seasons at St James' Park and his goals helped United win five league titles in his seven full seasons at Old Trafford.

Ferguson's best signing at United, and arguably pound-for-pound the best transfer of all time, would not have been allowed to go through if there had been transfer windows at the time. Eric Cantona moved from Leeds United to Manchester United for £1 million on 26 November 1992 – five weeks before the winter window now opens during January.

I was working at STV when Cantona had signed for Leeds United in February 1992. I was sent down to Leeds nine months later to interview Gary McAllister, because Rangers were playing Leeds in the Champions League and you won't be surprised to hear the games were being billed as 'The Battle of Britain'.

Clubs were much more open and welcoming in those days and the Leeds manager Howard Wilkinson kindly allowed me to watch the players train. I will never forget what I saw that day. There were some fantastic players on the pitch but time and time again my eyes were drawn to just one of them. Even if you knew nothing about football – and I am no stranger to that accusation over the years – you could see immediately that Cantona was an exceptional player. His touch and vision and finishing were there for all to see, even if it was just a training game.

For all his talents, Cantona was an idiosyncratic character and Wilkinson wasn't prepared to treat him any differently to his other players. Cantona helped Leeds win the title in May 1992 but there were problems off the pitch and, six months later, Wilkinson controversially allowed him to move to Manchester United. The deal only happened because Leeds chairman Bill Fotherby called his Manchester

United counterpart, Martin Edwards, to ask if he was interested in selling Denis Irwin to Leeds. Alex Ferguson happened to be in the room with Edwards at the time. Fotherby was told Irwin was not for sale but Ferguson was interested in Cantona if a deal could be done. A few days and just £1 million later, the Frenchman was a Manchester United player.

Ferguson and Cantona were made for each other and, long after they both retired, their names are still sung at United games. Cantona was the spark that really fired United back into life again. In his first season at Old Trafford, United won the title and they won it another three times in four seasons before Cantona retired at just thirty. He left the crowd wanting more, walking away from football because he felt it had become more of a business than a sport – lucky he is not around now.

It was a running joke at United during Cantona's five seasons at Old Trafford that Ferguson would let him get away with far more than other players. His teammates didn't mind because they knew how special Cantona was and how much he brought to the squad. There was no one better than Ferguson when it came to handling big-name players. He could read their minds, he knew what made them tick and he knew which buttons to press to make sure he got everything out of them for the good of the team. Very few people could have handled Cantona the way Ferguson did and there is still an incredible bond between the two men.

Three months after Cantona played his final game for United, Ferguson wrote a beautiful letter to him which you can find on the internet. Ferguson writes that United have started pre-season training again and he keeps waiting for Cantona to appear. He says he knows that is not going to happen because he knew Cantona's time was up from his eyes the last time they met. Ferguson and Cantona's father had tried to make him reconsider, but Ferguson then simply tells Cantona to make sure he stays fit and active. He also writes about how his replacement, Teddy Sheringham, has been finding it a little bit difficult to adapt to playing for United after leaving Spurs.

In the letter Ferguson also reveals that he had spoken to Cantona about United needing to sign a top-class striker but financial restraints at the club meant that they could not sign the best players. Ferguson sounds frustrated. He feels time is running out for him to win the European Cup – he is writing two years before he did exactly that with United at the Nou Camp in 1999 – and he says his dream is to discover a new Cantona.

In the penultimate paragraph, he invites Cantona to come and see him any time he wants, as a friend, just for a chat and a cup of tea, and he thanks him for his service to Manchester United. Ferguson signs off by writing: 'Eric, you know where I am if you need me and now that you are no longer one of my players, I hope you know you have a friend.'

One can only imagine what it was like for Cantona to receive and read a letter like that from Ferguson. It tells you a lot about the kind of man Ferguson is and the kind of player Cantona was. If there has ever been a better value for money transfer, I would love to know the name of the player and the clubs involved.

Although Ferguson signed lots of other exceptional players, it is no surprise that someone who was at the same club for twenty-six years made some bad buys and missed out on some great players during that time as well. All football fans of a certain age will know that Ferguson came agonisingly close to signing Paul Gascoigne. It is one of the biggest 'what ifs' of the English game.

What if Paul Gascoigne had signed for Manchester United instead of Tottenham Hotspur two years before the World Cup in Italy in 1990? Would Ferguson have been able to stop Gascoigne drinking during and after his career? Would Gascoigne have won it all and become an even better player than he turned out to be? Would he have avoided his terrible injury problems? Would Ferguson have helped him cope better with his personal issues? Who knows? What we do know is that if anyone in the game could have helped and managed Gascoigne it would have been Ferguson. He would have been a challenge even for Ferguson, quite possibly the biggest challenge of his career as far as managing a player was concerned. Ferguson would have kept a very close watch on him, he would have backed him in public and criticised and advised him in private when the time was right. He would have told him how much he valued him and he would have told him that he was always there if he needed him, no matter how he was feeling or what he was going through.

Could it have happened? Could Gascoigne have played for United? Very much so. Ferguson tried hard to sign him from Newcastle United in 1988 and he came very close to getting his man. Gascoigne was only twenty at the time and, even though he had not played for England yet, his advisers wanted him to be the best paid player at United on £2,500-a-week.

That was never going to happen, but after face-to-face talks Ferguson was confident he had convinced Gascoigne to sign for United. It was only while he was on holiday – allegedly relaxing by the pool – that Ferguson received the news he had been dreading. Gascoigne had met Spurs manager Terry Venables while Ferguson was on holiday in Malta and the meeting had gone well. So well, in fact, that Gascoigne decided to sign for Spurs.

'They signed him by buying his mum and dad a house in the north-east,' Ferguson said. 'Losing out on him was the biggest disappointment of all.'

Ferguson had every right to feel disappointed. When he was fit and well, Gascoigne was one of the best players in the world and he was a joy to watch. I remember being at Ibrox in April 1996 when he scored a hat-trick as Rangers won the title by beating Aberdeen 3–0. His first two goals were poetry in motion. He made it 1–0 by beating two desperate Aberdeen defenders before finishing with his right foot from an ever-decreasing angle on the left. In the second half, he won the ball in his own half and surged through Aberdeen's midfield and defence to make it 2–0 with his left foot.

When you saw Gascoigne put in those kinds of performances in crucial games which he won almost singlehandedly, there is no reason to doubt that he would have been a sensational signing for United. He is one of the best players I have seen and I believe he would have had a similar impact at United to Cantona, Cristiano Ronaldo and Wayne Rooney. That is how good Gascoigne was and he would have been even better if he had worked with Ferguson.

Of course, Ferguson didn't just miss out on Gascoigne. Another English legend he failed to sign was Alan Shearer and, to make matters worse, it happened twice. The first time was in 1992 when Shearer moved from Southampton to Blackburn Rovers. The second time was four years later when he moved to Newcastle United. Looking back, it doesn't seem like Ferguson could have done much more to get a deal done for Shearer in 1996. According to Martin Edwards, who was the United chairman at the time, Shearer had wanted to move to Old Trafford but Blackburn owner Jack Walker did not want to sell his star striker to his club's Lancashire rivals.

What is clear is that United were told that Shearer wanted to come to Old Trafford and his goals would have made a side who had just won the Double again even better. Talks were held with Shearer and his agent and all seemed to be going well until the agent called Ferguson and told him they had decided to sign for Newcastle instead.

Ferguson did his best to try and get over it by going on a shopping spree. He bought Ronny Johnsen, Jordi Cruyff, Karel Poborsky, Raimond van der Gouw and a young striker called Ole Gunnar Solskjær. The Norwegian with the baby face went on to win six titles, two FA Cups and the Champions League at Old Trafford. Shearer scored 148 times for Newcastle and, although he didn't win anything at St James' Park, it's impossible to put into words or measure in silverware the joy and pride he must have felt playing for his hometown club.

It might sound crazy, but even now when you go to St James' Park there seems to be an extra buzz in the ground if Shearer is there watching or working for TV or radio. He was a god to those supporters when he was playing and he is still a god to them now. If he hadn't played for Newcastle, we would have been deprived of one of the great love affairs of modern football, between Shearer and those incredible supporters.

Ferguson always liked having at least one supremely talented maverick in his United squads as well and they didn't come any more special or enigmatic than Paolo Di Canio. The unpredictable but sublimely talented Italian and United would have been a match made in heaven. It almost happened in January 2002, when Ferguson tried to sign Di Canio from West Ham United. According to Ferguson, the deal collapsed when Di Canio asked for too much money.

'I tried so hard to get Di Canio,' he said. 'The deal was all done. We had made an offer he had accepted, but then he came back saying he wanted more. We couldn't agree to the new demand.'

Di Canio remembers things differently and he says it didn't happen because he couldn't bear to turn his back on West Ham. Another theory why the deal fell through is that United needed to sell Dwight Yorke first, but he refused to join Middlesbrough.

Ferguson also tried and failed to sign Les Ferdinand when he was looking for a new striker in December 1994. Ferdinand had made a name for himself with his goals for Queens Park Rangers and they were ready to let him go for the right price.

Ferguson called Ray Wilkins, who had played with Ferdinand at QPR, to ask for a character reference. Wilkins had only good things to say, so United went ahead and made a bid. At the same time, Wilkins called Ferdinand and told him what had happened and said a bid was imminent.

Ferdinand went to see the QPR chairman, Richard Thompson, the next day. He was told he would be allowed to leave if he wanted. 'It's Manchester United,' Ferdinand said, believing a deal was now close. But that's when everything started to go wrong.

QPR manager Gerry Francis resigned when he found out Ferdinand was about to be sold. Thompson couldn't lose his manager and his star striker in the same week so he convinced Ferdinand to stay.

A few days later, Ferdinand was surprised to discover Wilkins was his new QPR manager. Wilkins had accepted Thompson's job offer on one condition – that Ferdinand was not sold. 'You've learned an important lesson,' Wilkins told Ferdinand after his United move failed to materialise. 'In this game, you have to look after number one.'

It must have hurt Ferguson to miss out on players like Gascoigne, Shearer and Ferdinand, although knowing the man, not for long, and it was the same story with Gareth Bale, a player who went on to win the Champions League four times at Real Madrid. Long before anyone in Madrid had taken any notice of Bale, Ferguson tried to sign him for United in 2007. There was talk of a £4 million offer when Bale was coming up through the ranks at Southampton, but he ended up moving to Tottenham. Bale says he chose Spurs because he thought he would play more regularly at White Hart Lane, but Ferguson blamed Southampton. 'It was not the boy who turned us down,' Ferguson said. 'It was Southampton.'

I met Bale a few times when he was at Tottenham but I am not sure he was delighted to spend part of his Christmas Day with me one year. Professional players in the UK often play on Boxing Day and that means training on Christmas Day. On that particular 25 December, I drove up to Spurs Lodge, Tottenham's former training ground in Chigwell, to interview their manager, Harry Redknapp. It had become a bit of an annual tradition for me to interview Harry on Christmas Day and it was a good way for me to get out of the house nice and early and get some fresh air before the rest of the day's festivities or, sometimes, work.

After I had finished interviewing Harry, I asked him if there was any chance of a word with Gareth. You would think Premier League players would have better things to do on Christmas Day than stand outside in the cold talking to me, but that was not the case with Bale. He was more than happy to talk as long as I wanted, even though he probably had his whole family and a turkey waiting at home.

Just a few years later in 2013, I was very lucky to know people close to him who gave me the inside track when I was reporting on his long drawn out dream move from Tottenham to Real Madrid. He had always wanted to play for Real Madrid and I am delighted for him that he won so many trophies there. During his time in Spain he was frequently linked with a move to United, but I was always told there was no chance that he would leave Madrid until his contract ran out in 2022.

As far as Ferguson was concerned, there were no hard feelings about missing out on Bale. You win some and you lose some and it's not just forwards Ferguson had to get over not signing. In 2003, he went on a scouting mission to France to watch a young goalkeeper playing for Rennes. He had received glowing reports about the player and it was now time for a personal check on a Czech called Petr Čech.

Ferguson was impressed but not convinced that Čech was what United were looking for at the time. 'He was eighteen or nineteen,' Ferguson said. 'I told myself he was too young for us.' He wasn't too young for Chelsea when they signed him a year later for £7 million. You don't need me to tell you that Čech went on to establish himself as one of the best goalkeepers in the world during eleven seasons at Stamford Bridge, and he left for Arsenal in 2015 after winning four titles, four FA Cups, three League Cups, the Europa League and the Champions League at Chelsea.

A player who won even more than Čech and who – you guessed it – United also failed to sign was the one and only Zinedine Zidane. In the summer of 1996 it was an open secret in football that Zidane would be leaving Bordeaux. He had just become Player of the Year in France and he was being watched by scouts from all the biggest clubs in Europe.

United had him on their list of targets and Eric Cantona told Ferguson that he should sign him. According to former United chairman Martin Edwards, United didn't make a move for Zidane because Ferguson thought he was not what they needed at the time. Zidane swapped Bordeaux for Juventus in a £3 million deal that summer and went on to win some of the game's biggest trophies with Juventus, Real Madrid and France. Ferguson didn't do too badly without him either, but it would have been truly special for United and English football if Zidane had moved to England instead of Italy when he was twenty-four.

Fast forward seven years to the summer of 2003, and United fans' emotions were all over the place as David Beckham was sold to Real Madrid and United were apparently close to signing Brazilian sensation Ronaldinho.

The only problem was that Barcelona were also desperate to sign Ronaldinho after missing out on Beckham, so it came as no surprise when he was seen juggling a ball at the Nou Camp after a €30 million deal had been agreed with Paris Saint-Germain. All was not lost for United though. Later that summer, they signed Cristiano Ronaldo from Sporting Lisbon for £12 million and they even managed to buy a Brazilian as well – Kléberson.

You need to be a little bit older to remember when United missed out on a player who went on to have a glittering career at their arch rivals Liverpool.

'Catch me if you can. Cause I'm a United man. And what you're looking at is the master plan.'

Don't laugh, John Barnes really could have worn the red of United instead of the red of Liverpool. United were interested in signing him before he moved to Liverpool in 1987 and Ferguson has admitted he made a mistake by not trying to do a deal. But perhaps we shouldn't be too hard on Ferguson because it was United's scouts at the time who were not convinced that Barnes was right for United and, in any case, Danish winger Jesper Olsen had just signed a new long-term deal at Old Trafford. Ferguson regretted not signing Barnes but the player never looked back. In his first season at Liverpool he won the title and he was named PFA Player of the Year.

Reading all these names of players Ferguson missed out on may leave you with the impression that he didn't know what he was doing in the transfer market. Nothing could be further from the truth. You could write a whole book about all the great players Ferguson signed during his extraordinary career.

As a rule of thumb, and a very unscientific one at that, if you are a manager and 50 per cent of the players you sign turn out to be good deals then you are doing pretty well. Nobody can deny what a great operator Ferguson was in the market and you could make a pretty compelling case that he did not always have the financial firepower that some of his European rivals had when it came to buying players. Ferguson's teams were a blend of players United had developed and players they signed.

Yes, Ferguson missed out on players like Gascoigne, Shearer and Bale but you can't really argue with the record of a manager who signed Cristiano Ronaldo, Wayne Rooney, Eric Cantona, Peter Schmeichel, Roy Keane, Ruud van Nistelrooy, Rio Ferdinand, Nemanja Vidić, Denis Irwin, Jaap Stam and Dimitar Berbatov. I could go on and on and on but I think you get my drift.

Transfers are just like love – it's better to have tried and failed to sign a great player than to have never tried at all. All great managers have their share of players they missed out on and Ferguson's greatest rival during the Premier League era was no different. When you think of Arsène Wenger and transfers your mind immediately starts conjuring up images of players like Thierry Henry, Patrick Vieira, Robert Pires and Marc Overmars. Wenger signed some incredible players at incredible prices and the move from Highbury to the

Emirates Stadium meant he had to operate with one hand tied behind his back for years, because of financial constraints associated with building the new ground.

Wenger took it all in his stride and, although he may have stayed at Arsenal a little bit too long, nobody can argue with his impact on the English game and his eye for an exceptional player. You could write a whole book about all the great players he signed and, just like Ferguson, you can write a long list of all the great players he tried and failed to sign.

Some of the players Wenger missed out on are well known, some of the deals that failed to happen are more surprising. For instance, when you picture David Ginola in a football shirt you see him in the white of Spurs or the black and white stripes of Newcastle United but it could have been the red of Arsenal.

Ginola and his long, lustrous locks used to star in a famous shampoo commercial on TV. His catchphrase was, 'Because I'm worth it.' In 1995, Arsenal thought he was worth it, but so did Barcelona and Newcastle. Ginola had just won the title with Paris Saint-Germain and he was the French Player of the Year. He was available for £2.5 million. Barcelona manager Johann Cruyff wanted him but he had to sell Hristo Stoichkov and Gheorghe Hagi first. Ginola had his heart set on the Nou Camp, but when it became apparent that they could not sell Stoichkov and Hagi, Kevin Keegan convinced him to sign for Newcastle.

Ginola was about to sign for Newcastle when he got a late-night call from Arsenal. They wanted him at Highbury.

'I had given my word to Newcastle,' Ginola said, speaking to *FourFourTwo* magazine in 2015. 'I went there.' In any case, in the long run, Wenger and Arsenal didn't do too badly without Ginola and he became an instant hero at Newcastle as they went close to winning the title for the first time in sixty-nine years.

It's now hard to imagine Ginola wearing Arsenal's famous red and white kit and it's just as hard trying to imagine Jamie Vardy wearing it. Vardy is Mr Leicester City, the striker whose goals helped them win that incredible title in the summer of 2016. Just a few weeks after that stunning achievement, it really did look like Vardy was going to be on his way to Arsenal.

From non-League to Premier League, Vardy's is some story, as is the story about a potential move to Arsenal. Just how close it was to happening depends on whose version you prefer. Vardy says he never spoke to Wenger after Arsenal had triggered his release clause. Vardy had 'unfinished business' at Leicester and it was an 'easy decision' to stay.

Arsenal's transfer negotiator at the time, Dick Law, remembered things differently. 'The deal with Leicester was done, the deal with the player was done,' Law said, speaking to the *Athletic* in 2020. 'He came down to visit with his wife Rebekah. He sat on the couch in front of Arsène, and then he backed off. On his way back to Leicester, I get a call from the player saying he wants to think about it overnight. At that point, you know it's bad news.' Sure enough, a few days later, Vardy signed a new contract at Leicester.

Vardy is a man of few words who prefers to do his talking on the pitch. Nobody can take away that amazing title achievement with Leicester and his twenty-four league goals that season are just one of the reasons he is so loved by their fans. Strikers are the most precious commodity in the transfer market because goals win games, and a finisher with an even better scoring record than Vardy is Luis Suárez.

'What do you think they're smoking over there at Emirates?'

Liverpool owner John Henry's ten-word question is one of the most famous football tweets. It was almost midnight on 23 July 2013 when Henry reached for his phone and typed out his response to Arsenal's attempt to sign Liverpool's star striker Luis Suárez. Arsenal had just made a £40,000,001 bid for Suárez and that rogue pound has become legendary in football history.

Wenger has since claimed Suárez wanted the move, but admitted Arsenal had misunderstood the clause in his Liverpool contract. The £40 million wasn't a release clause. It was simply a clause that allowed Suárez to talk to another club. The Uruguayan did leave Liverpool the following summer. Unfortunately for Arsenal, he went to Barcelona. For £75 million.

I've always found Suárez to be a strangely compelling character. I think it has something to do with that strange mix of extraordinary talent and the side of his character which always seems to place him right at the centre of controversy. Some of the scrapes he got into almost had a funny side, some of them were very serious.

I tried to find out more about him and his background when I was in South America in the summer of 2014. I was having dinner in São Paolo with an agent and he told me to go to Montevideo to speak to some people he could put me in touch with who were close to Suárez. Thanks to him, I spent a magical few days in Uruguay's capital and one of the highlights was speaking to Suárez's former teammates, coaches and friends at his first club, Nacional. I also made a short film about Suárez and Uruguay, and I was so pleased with it that I decided to see if I could give him a copy when I got back to England.

Before the new season started, I arranged to meet Suárez at Liverpool's training ground and I gave him a DVD of the film. I also took along a Nacional shirt which he kindly signed for me. Four years later, I met him again after he had played for Barcelona against Chelsea at Stamford Bridge. I think he liked the film because he greeted me warmly and told everyone within earshot that I was the 'man who loves Uruguay.'

So Arsenal missed out on Suárez and they also missed out on Didier Drogba. Don't laugh because it really could have happened. And yes, we are talking about the same Drogba who seemed to love nothing more than scoring against Arsenal. It must have hurt Wenger to admit it but he has said he turned down the chance to sign Drogba from Le Mans for just £100,000 in 2004.

'I would have loved to manage Drogba for two reasons,' Wenger said, speaking at an Arsenal corporate event in 2014.

'One, I missed him when he played at Le Mans. I knew there was a good player there and I missed him. And secondly, because he hurt us so much in big games that all this pain would not have happened.'

Another player who caused Wenger a lot of pain was Cristiano Ronaldo and, you guessed it, Wenger tried to sign him as well. Now, 6 August 2003 will go down as a significant day in the history of Manchester United. Sporting Lisbon celebrated the opening of their new stadium with a pre-season match against the English champions. It was the game when Ronaldo ran United ragged and it was the performance which convinced Ferguson that he had to sign the teenager as quickly as possible. Within a week, Ronaldo moved to Old Trafford after United agreed to pay Sporting £12 million. But things could have been very different. So much so that we could easily be talking about the Arsenal legend Cristiano Ronaldo. 'It's true. Very close,' Ronaldo said when asked if he could have joined Arsenal. 'Seriously. It didn't happen but Arsenal, I appreciate what they did for me. Especially Arsène Wenger.'

Ronaldo is an absolute gentleman when you meet him, or should I say *if* you meet him, because getting close to him is not easy. My colleague Piers Morgan got a brilliant scoop and exclusive interview with Ronaldo which led to him leaving United for the second time at the end of 2022. Some of the things Ronaldo said about United left a bad taste in the mouth and it was a shame to see such a great player leaving such a great club in those circumstances. Having said that, I thought Erik ten Hag handled the situation very well and he sent out a very strong message about who is in charge at United.

I interviewed Ronaldo a few times when he was at the top of his game, trading goals and Ballon d'Or awards with his great rival, Lionel Messi. One of my most memorable encounters with him ended up with him signing my shoes. I feel like I should explain here that I was not wearing them at the time and they were a pair of brand new trainers which I later auctioned off at a charity dinner for £3,000.

Life is full of sliding doors moments and football is no different. There are plenty of occasions in the past when things could have turned out very differently. For example, a certain Sir Alex Ferguson really could have managed Arsenal. Close your eyes and imagine Fergie at Highbury. All those titles. All those European Cups. It did almost happen twice, in 1983 and in 1986.

In 1983, Arsenal needed a new manager after Terry Neill was sacked. Ferguson had led Aberdeen to victory against Real Madrid in the European Cup Winners' Cup final in Gothenburg and he was an outstanding candidate. He said all the right things as well. 'I think Arsenal are the most glamorous team,' he told the *Sun* in December 1983. Nevertheless, he decided to stay in Scotland and wait for another opportunity to move to England.

That came again three years later and it was Arsenal again. They offered him the chance to take over from Don

Howe and they wanted a quick answer. Ferguson met the Arsenal board but, according to his account, they did not see eye to eye. He decided to stay at Aberdeen until the Manchester United job became available in November 1986. You don't need me to tell you how much he won at Old Trafford but in case anyone has forgotten it was twenty-five major trophies including thirteen league titles and two European Cups.

It would be interesting to see how Ferguson and his great rival Wenger would have fared in the modern transfer market now that the top players and their agents have become so powerful. The very best players now don't want to be bought and sold by clubs without them having a lot of control over the deals and their own career development. When you are as good as Erling Haaland, Kylian Mbappé or Jude Bellingham, you now have the power to control every move in your career. You can do that by making sure you have release clauses in your contract or by only signing shorter term contracts, say for two or three years instead of the more standard four- or five-year deals.

If you have signed only a three-year deal, after one season you will just have two years left on your contract and your club will have to consider selling you or offering you a new deal, because your price in the market will decrease as your contract runs down towards the end date when you can leave as a free agent. Having a release clause in your contract gives you a lot of power as well and it can help you plan your career and use clubs as stepping stones towards your ultimate destination during the peak years of your career.

Haaland is a great example of what you can do now if you are as good as he is. He is a player who has managed his career perfectly and benefited all parties every time he has moved, although not as much as some of them would have wanted. When he moved from Molde in Norway to Red Bull Salzburg in Austria in 2019, his agents made sure he had a €22.5 million release clause in his contract.

Borussia Dortmund activated the clause eighteen months later and, again, his agents made sure he had a release clause in his contract at the German club. Two and a half years later, Manchester City beat off fierce competition from all their European rivals to sign him after agreeing to activate his €60 million clause.

By insisting on having release clauses in his contract, Haaland's advisers made sure they and the player, not the selling club, had control over his career. If there had been no release clause in his Dortmund contract, the German club could have spent the summer of 2022 playing interested clubs off each other and they could probably have held out for a price not far off twice the €60 million clause, or they could have decided not to sell at all. That clause gave Haaland all the power. If he wanted to move to City, there was nothing anyone could do about it as long as City were willing to pay the clause, his wages and his representatives.

That was a no-brainer as far as City were concerned and hats off to them for getting the deal done because Haaland has turned out to be everything they could have wished for and more. He is quite simply one of the greatest strikers the world has ever seen and it's almost frightening to imagine what he can achieve in all the years he has ahead of him.

Of course, Haaland has been in a relatively special position when it comes to managing and developing his career. Not every player is as good and as sought after, and not every player can dictate to clubs what he wants in his contract. If you are not absolutely top quality, there is no way a club is going to agree to let you have a relatively modest release clause in your contract. They don't want to lose you on the cheap and they want to decide who to sell you to, when and for how much, rather than being forced to sell you for a pre-agreed set price, often at a set time.

Some big clubs also refuse to have release clauses in their players' contracts and that is rumoured to be one of the reasons why Manchester United missed out on signing Haaland, especially when he moved from Salzburg to Dortmund in 2020.

The view from the very top of the game must be very pleasant if you are as good as Haaland. For everyone else involved in the transfer market, life goes on. Players have to perform under intense pressure and scrutiny to keep their place in the team or to get a new contract or a move when the window opens again.

Agents have to work around the clock, making sure their clients are happy and settled and sorting out problems when things go wrong. They also have to devote a lot of their time to finding new players to represent as well as holding on to the ones they already have.

As for managers, they probably have the most difficult job of all when it comes to transfers. They are the ones who will get all the blame if things go wrong and nobody will forget if they sign a bad player.

These days there are a lot more people involved in transfers at clubs as well. There are big recruitment departments and armies of data analysts and scouts working hard to try and find the perfect player for the right price for their clubs.

Of course, legendary managers like Ferguson and Wenger worked with scouts, recruitment specialists and senior club executives as well, but you always had the sense that they were the ones making the big calls. Modern managers have many more tools at their disposal when it comes to finding players, they have more data, more video and more staff to help them, but at the end of the day it can just come down to having a good eye for a player.

That is just one of the many qualities that Ferguson and Wenger both had. They signed some incredible players and they both missed out on some good ones. When you are judging their buys, never forget that they operated when things were very different to the way they are now. For long stretches of their careers they were restricted, in relative terms, when it came to how much money they could spend on players. In the modern era, Premier League clubs can outbid and outspend and pay higher wages than almost all their European rivals. That was certainly not the case when

Ferguson was in charge of United and Wenger was in charge of Arsenal. In those days, clubs like Real Madrid, Barcelona, Juventus, AC Milan and Inter Milan were richer and had much more pulling power when it came to signing the best players in the world. That makes what Ferguson and Wenger achieved even more remarkable.

Chapter 7

Artificial Intelligence

To be a good journalist you have to talk to people. To get stories you have be interested in them and listen to what they say. In that respect, life as a football reporter is getting more and more difficult because meaningful access and interaction with players, managers, owners and agents is becoming rarer and rarer. You may get the opportunity to ask a player or a manager a question at regular set-piece press conferences, but you usually get only one question and the answers in those environments tend to be guarded and noncommittal.

It can be different if you are a news journalist. If you are sent to cover a big breaking news story there is a good chance you will find eyewitnesses who will want to speak to you and tell you what has happened. It is the same if you are a political reporter at Westminster where there are hundreds of MPs, Lords, special advisers and lobbyists who you can approach, get to know and cultivate as contacts.

That's much more difficult to do in modern football because people will usually only speak to you if they are contractually obliged to – and even then they will not want to give too much away. There is a way around this problem though. All you need to do is be a bloody good journalist. If someone puts an obstacle in your way you just have to find a way to overcome it. If you are the kind of person who just takes no for an answer, you are not going to break any stories. It takes a lot of hard work and persistence to break stories. Actors don't stop going to auditions because they keep getting turned down for roles and you have to have the same mindset. You have to believe in yourself and what you are doing. It might take years of asking before you get that big interview you have always wanted, it might take months and months of phone calls, messages and emails. People will keep saying no and you have to take all the rejections in your stride. In my experience, nine times out of ten persistence will eventually pay off.

One way to get around the access problem is to look for interesting characters and stories further down the football pyramid. If you are starting out as a sports journalist, it is going to be extremely tough for you to break big transfer stories so you may be better off keeping an eye out for the weird and the wonderful in the lower leagues.

That is what I did in 2002 and it led to me getting to know one of the most colourful characters I have ever come across in football. It would be an understatement to describe George Reynolds as a larger-than-life character. Reynolds led an extraordinary life before he died in 2021 at the age of eighty-four. From an early age, he was in trouble with the law and he served a six-month prison sentence in the 1960s for theft. Soon after he was released, he made a name for himself in the underworld as a safecracker, utilising the training he had received handling explosives in coal mines to blow up safes during robberies. Reynolds was in and out of prison during the 1960s and 1970s until he decided to go straight by setting up a kitchen building business. This made him one of the richest men in the UK with a fortune estimated by the *Sunday Times* in 2000 to be worth £260 million.

You may be wondering what this all has to do with football and transfers. Well, the answer is pretty simple. Reynolds, like many rich men, decided to buy a football club. What made Reynolds different to other rich men who have bought clubs is his background in crime, his unique way of doing business and the fact that he wasn't really a football fan. Reynolds bought Darlington when they were about to go out of business in 1999. They were in the old Division Three when he bought them, which was the fourth tier of English football at the time. He had grandiose plans – don't they all – and he said he was going to turn them into a Premier League club. Despite building a new £20 million stadium, which he named after himself, it all ended in tears four years later when the club went into administration.

Who knows if things might have turned out differently if Reynolds had managed to pull off one of the most surprising transfers of all time, when he came close to signing former

Newcastle United and Colombia forward Faustino Asprilla? Reynolds thought he had the deal in the bag, so much so that Asprilla was paraded in front of the fans before Darlington's home game against Carlisle United on 27 August 2002.

Even though Darlington were playing in the bottom division at the time, it was a big transfer story and luckily I had got to know Reynolds when he bought the club and announced his grand plans. Although you had to be careful not to get on his wrong side, Reynolds was approachable and straight-talking whenever I contacted him to talk about his club. He had no problem with me having his number but I don't think I ever got one of his famous business cards which introduced him as 'George Reynolds, managing director, chairman, gentleman, entrepreneur, adventurer, maker of money and utter genius.'

I called Reynolds when I was told by a contact based in the north-east that Darlington were trying to sign Asprilla. He was still only thirty-two and he was a free agent at that stage of his career. He had left Newcastle in 1998 and, after playing in Italy, Brazil and Mexico, he had been back in the north-east to watch Newcastle play in a pre-season friendly at St James' Park. That is where he had first met Reynolds and that is when Reynolds came up with the crazy idea of signing him for Darlington.

Reynolds was prepared to break the bank for Asprilla and he told me he had offered the player a house and a luxury car as well as a two-year contract reported to be worth

£17,000 a week. All Asprilla had to do was agree to play for a team who had finished fifteenth in English football's basement division the previous season. Asprilla appeared to be happy to do that and he also seemed to find the terms on offer acceptable. Darlington were so convinced they had signed Asprilla that he was even listed as one of their players in the Kidderminster Harriers programme for their home game against Darlington on 31 August.

In fact, the move was so advanced Reynolds even agreed to talk about it in a live TV interview outside his £7 million Georgian mansion. Halfway through the interview, a red Renault appeared and Asprilla got out, hugged Reynolds and started answering questions from the reporter about his big move. Asprilla seemed happy and relaxed and he was looking forward to making his Darlington debut. There was even talk of him sticking around long enough to lead the club into the Premier League at their new stadium.

Reynolds was offering Asprilla an extraordinary deal but unfortunately it turned out to be not good enough. Just two days after he had been paraded in front of the Darlington fans, I got another call from my north-east contact who told me he had heard Asprilla had failed to turn up for his medical and had last been seen boarding a flight to the Middle East.

I called Reynolds straight away and he took the call even though he was right in the middle of eating his dinner. 'What's happened, George?' I said. 'Where's Tino? Why didn't he have his medical today? You said you'd signed him. You paraded him in front of the fans.' There was silence on the line for a few seconds before Reynolds cleared his throat. 'He's fucked off, Jim.'

And that was that. One of the most surprising transfers of all time fell apart at the last minute because one of the parties involved had a change of heart. I say change of heart but, more often than not, when transfers fall apart it has more to do with money than heart. I can't be sure, but I would hazard a pretty good guess that Asprilla would have signed on the dotted line at Darlington if the money had been right. Speaking to *FourFourTwo* magazine six years after the move had collapsed, he explained that all had not been what it had seemed and the wages which had been agreed verbally didn't turn out to be the wages which were written down in the contract he was asked to sign. 'On the phone I was given one contract,' Asprilla said. 'In person he gave me another.'

You can't criticise Asprilla for not signing if he felt the terms of the deal were not right, especially because he was being asked to drop down to play in the fourth tier. Footballers have a relatively short career and they have to maximise what they earn before they usually retire in their mid-thirties. Like it or not, and I'm not sure I do, football has become a business and everyone is looking out for themselves. Reynolds was trying to do what he thought was best for Reynolds and Darlington; Asprilla was doing what was best for Asprilla.

There was never a dull moment when Reynolds was around but the way he ran Darlington ended up having serious repercussions for the club. They went into administration three times between 2003 and 2012 and are currently playing in the sixth tier in the National League North. I didn't stay in touch with Reynolds after Darlington went into administration in 2003. The next time I heard about him was in 2005, when he was sentenced to three years in prison for tax evasion after police found £500,000 in the boot of his car.

There were some big money moves in the 2002 summer transfer window. Manchester United signed Rio Ferdinand for £30 million from Leeds United and Manchester City paid Paris Saint-Germain £13 million for Nicolas Anelka. But the deal that I remember most from that summer is the one that didn't happen, and the one that would have been one of the most surprising transfers of all time if it had gone through – Faustino Asprilla to Darlington.

That failed move shows that you can find some great stories and great contacts in the lower leagues. It is always going to be difficult for a reporter to get to know the owners of the big clubs, especially when you are starting out, but the lower you go the more you will find that people are willing to give you the time of day.

I don't want to be disrespectful here to anyone who plays or works in the so-called lower leagues. I'm not even particularly comfortable using that phrase. There are great players and managers and owners and people working throughout the football pyramid. I enjoy watching games at all levels. Of course, I'm never there just to enjoy myself; in the back of my mind, I'm always looking for a story and I'm always looking for contacts.

The Championship is one of the most competitive leagues in the world and it is full of great stories and colourful characters. One story that really caught my eye in 2010 was when a Malaysian billionaire businessman called Vincent Tan took control of Cardiff City by buying a 36 per cent stake in the Championship club. Tan made some bizarre decisions at Cardiff, including changing their famous blue shirts to red in order to 'appeal to international markets.' Within three years of Tan's arrival, Cardiff were in the Premier League and, luckily, by then I had managed to add him to my list of contacts.

What I really wanted was an exclusive interview with Tan and, after a few calls and messages in the autumn of 2014, I was finally told I could meet him in person as long as I went to Malaysia. Before anyone could change their mind, I was on a thirteen-hour flight from London to Kuala Lumpur with a cameraman. I wasn't 100 per cent sure that the interview was going to happen but I figured out it would be much more difficult for Tan to have a change of heart once he knew I had travelled 6,500 miles to meet him.

I should not have worried about anyone standing me up. As soon as we checked into our hotel in the Malaysian capital I received a text message asking me to be on the roof of our hotel after breakfast the next day. After finishing our corn flakes and cups of tea the following morning, the cameraman and I got the lift up to our hotel roof where we found a helicopter waiting to take us to the interview.

By this stage, I was beginning to feel like I was in a Bond movie and that sense only heightened when I was told we were flying to meet Tan on his yacht somewhere in the South China Sea. Now, I don't know much about helicopters and I know very little about yachts. I guess that's why I was wondering to myself how big Tan's yacht would have to be for us to land on it safely. I needn't have worried because about twenty minutes later we landed on Tan's private island. Twenty-four hours earlier I had been sitting in a cold and wet London and here I was swooping around south-east Asia in a billionaire's helicopter on the way to a secret meeting.

I was having one of the most enjoyable days of my career, and things went from great to even better when we landed on the island and were told that the final leg of our journey would be on a tender that was waiting to take us to Tan's yacht. We had been treated like royalty ever since we landed in Malaysia and we received a welcome fit for a king when we boarded Tan's $50 million yacht.

I had never met Tan before and I did not know what to expect. I should not have worried. He was hugely courteous and very welcoming considering he had never met me before and he could not be sure about my motives for wanting to speak to him. I will never forget the sight of Tan appearing to greet us wearing dark sunglasses and a red Cardiff home shirt with 'Visit Malaysia' written across the front.

Before the interview, Tan insisted that we had lunch with him and he was great company during the meal. He was happy to talk about anything and everything and he was just as open and honest when the camera started rolling. I have to admit, I did feel a little bit sorry for the cameraman because filming an interview and keeping a steady shot is not easy when you're on a boat that's bobbing around in the sea.

With the interview in the bag, we had dinner and a few drinks – soft ones for me – before we said our goodbyes as we would be leaving early the following morning. I remember lying in my cabin that night on a billionaire's yacht with a big smile on my face even though I had no idea where I really was. All I knew was that we were somewhere near Malaysia. Anyway, before I knew it, my alarm went off at 6 a.m. and we set off to do the same journey in reverse all the way back to London.

The interview generated a lot of interest and headlines because Tan was one of the most controversial figures in English football at the time. Unfortunately, Cardiff were relegated from the Premier League in 2014 and again in 2019. They have been struggling back in the Championship at the time of writing and they seem to have a revolving door when it comes to managers.

I still try and stay in contact with Tan and I think of him whenever I look out for Cardiff's results. The only way to get stories in this business is to stay in touch and maintain your relationships with the people who matter. It will not always be possible to make contact with the people at the biggest clubs, but in the football world there are stories everywhere and as a journalist it is your job to get out there and find them. If an owner or a player or a manager is making a name for himself outside the Premier League, it can often be the perfect opportunity for you to get to know them. Grab the chance while you can because they will be much more difficult to get hold of if they make it all the way to the top.

The more people you know in football, the more stories you will be able to break. The football media ecosystem is full of people talking about transfers. Everyone seems to have an opinion but, at the end of the day, the only currencies that really matter are facts and news. If you can get to know the people who are involved in deals and you gain their trust, you will have access to priceless information which will help you break stories.

One of the criticisms that is often directed at transfer reporters is that what they are writing or talking about is just gossip and rumours. That can sting when you are a journalist who has been working hard all summer and winter trying to provide the most accurate information possible for your readers, viewers and listeners.

It can be especially frustrating because you cannot answer back truthfully and explain to people why they are wrong when they accuse you of knowing nothing about a deal you have been writing or talking about. As a reporter, you cannot reveal who you have been talking to because to reveal the identity of your source or sources would break one of the golden rules of journalism. You just have to let the criticism roll over you and play the long game. There is nothing you can do. If what you have written or said turns out to be true, hardly anyone will remember you. If it turns out to be wrong, you will be criticised. The best reporters make sure that they are never wrong by speaking to the very top people involved in deals and by having the best contacts who they trust and have known for a long time.

One of the most popular places for people to get the latest transfer news is a page on the BBC Sport website. To get to it you have to go to the football section of the site and click on the 'gossip' tab. Once you have done that, you will be taken to a page headlined 'rumours' which is updated every day. It is a round-up of all the latest transfer headlines from multiple outlets around the world and the newspapers, websites, TV and radio stations where the stories come from are credited in brackets.

Some football journalists don't like the page because they feel that it is aggregating transfer stories and encouraging people to look in one place for the latest updates, instead of looking at different sources like their own newspapers and websites where a lot of the stories come from. I think one of the other things that upsets some reporters is the use of the words 'rumours' and 'gossip'. Journalism is a tough job and, despite what many people think, it can be a hard life. Many people in the industry are constantly worried about losing their jobs, and pay, especially at entry level, can be very low. Keeping all that in mind, it is really not surprising that some people may take issue with their work being labelled 'rumours' and 'gossip'.

The *Cambridge Dictionary* defines 'rumour' as 'an unofficial, interesting story or piece of news that might be true or invented and quickly spreads from person to person'. Meanwhile, the same dictionary defines 'gossip' as 'conversations or reports about other people's private lives that might be unkind, disapproving, or not true'.

When you actually look up the definitions of 'rumour' and 'gossip' you can see why journalists don't like their work being described in those terms. Of course, football is a gossipy world; from top to bottom people are passing information and stories around. It is exactly the same with transfers. Everybody is talking about what they have heard and sharing information about numerous players and clubs.

However, rumours are not the currency that journalists deal in; they seek out the real news and the real facts and if you don't believe me, all you have to do is look up an old 'Gossip' and 'Rumours' page on the BBC website and see if the stories turned out to be true. I have just tried this unscientific experiment for myself and the results are very interesting. Totally at random, I used an internet search engine to find one of the old pages and it came up with the one for 15 May 2021. The headline is 'Transfer Rumours: Sancho, Varane, Salah, Konaté, Haaland, Andersen' and the first story, credited to Eurosport, is about Jadon Sancho:

'Sources close to Borussia Dortmund forward Jadon Sancho, twenty-one, are more confident than ever before that the England international will complete a move to Manchester United this summer. The Premier League club are expected to make an initial offer of £65–75 million.'

Of course, Eurosport were not the only outlet who had been reporting United's longstanding interest in Sancho and it's no surprise the story was spot-on because, months later, Sancho moved from Dortmund to United in a £73 million deal. In all, there are twenty-one stories on the page and another three of them are also about United. Two are about their interest in France centre-back Raphaël Varane, who was playing for Real Madrid at the time. The *Manchester Evening News* report United are holding talks with Real Madrid about the player and the *Daily Mirror* say United are set to make a £40 million bid for Varane. I'm sure you don't need me to tell you that two and a half months later, United signed Varane in a deal that was worth up to £42 million.

The *Sun* are also quoted as reporting that Sergio Agüero would leave Manchester City when his contract expired in a few weeks and he would take a pay cut to sign for Barcelona. Of course, the *Sun* story was right – Agüero said his good-byes to City and Barcelona announced on 31 May that they had agreed a deal for him to join them when his City contract ran out on 31 July.

Looking back now, almost everything that was reported turned out to be accurate. Some of the deals didn't happen but no one was reporting that they were definitely going to go through. In some instances, there were reports about a club showing an interest in a particular player – Southampton and Ruben Loftus-Cheek for example. Loftus-Cheek stayed at Chelsea but the interest from Southampton was very real.

I am a fan of the BBC and I am not having a go at them here. I think it's a valuable service to round up all the day's transfer news in one place, but at the same time I can also understand why some journalists are unhappy about their stories being used in this way. I can also understand why people may feel that it's a little bit disrespectful for their work to appear on a page about rumours and gossip. There are many excellent transfer reporters out there working very hard to find out the latest information, and I can assure you that what they are writing are not 'interesting stories or pieces of news that might be true or invented' and they are not 'conversations or reports about other people's private lives that might be unkind, disapproving, or not true.'

The *Financial Times* is a daily business newspaper which was founded in 1888. It is a serious newspaper for serious people and, if you read its famous pink pages or subscribe to its website, it marks you out as someone who works in banking, someone who is well off or both. Something very strange happened to the *Financial Times* on Friday 15 October 2021. For the first time in its 133-year history it had a transfer story on its front page – or should I say a transfer rumour? Of course, there had been thousands of stories about sterling on its front pages before but this was the first one about Raheem.

Manchester City footballer Raheem Sterling has told the *Financial Times* of his desire to leave the English Premier League champions, setting up what could be the sport's next potential blockbuster transfer.

The story was written by the paper's former sports editor, Murad Ahmed, who had been speaking to Sterling at the FT Business of Sport US Summit. Sterling spoke about his frustration at not starting games regularly at Manchester City and said he was open to the idea of moving to a different club.

Perhaps the *Financial Times* should consider putting more transfer stories on its front page, because what they reported turned out to be totally true. A year later, Sterling moved from City to Chelsea in a £50 million deal.

Football has become a big business and the *Financial Times* is one of the business papers of record. It has reported on many football stories in the past but they have tended to be about the business of football. When they have covered transfers, it has been to mark some of the biggest deals in the game. For example, Neymar and Lionel Messi moving to Paris Saint-Germain or Cristiano Ronaldo moving to Saudi Arabia. The Sterling story was the first time that I had seen an exclusive-style transfer story on its front page. It was such a good story I think I even saw it on the BBC transfer gossip and rumours page the next day.

Although the *Financial Times* may have decided that their readers are occasionally interested in big-money transfer stories, you won't find the kind of non-stop commentary that you will find on the big deals on social media throughout the summer and winter windows. It is a transfer phenomenon one of my colleagues calls 'Artificial Intelligence'. What he means by that is there are sometimes a lot of people writing about transfers when they might not have anything at all new to say. As a general rule of thumb, only a few well-connected journalists are going to be in contact with the major players on a big deal. Most of the time, the major players will not be in a position to provide a running commentary on what is happening and that creates an information vacuum.

That vacuum is then filled, according to my colleague, with people recycling news which many people will already know. Everyone can see the difference between a story or update which has new information and one which is really nothing more than a synopsis of information which is already out there, sprinkled with a bit of opinion. My colleague thinks there is a lot of Artificial Intelligence out there, especially during the summer, when a few big potential deals tend to dominate the transfer conversation.

I am going to sit on the fence on this one and say I am not sure I agree with my colleague. As ever, I think there are two sides to every story. On the one hand, of course, it can be frustrating to spend time reading, watching or listening to something which doesn't tell you anything new, but on the other hand I can understand why the media has to respond to the appetite for transfer stories by providing as much information and analysis as possible. And don't forget nobody is forcing anyone to read or watch or listen to anything they don't want to consume. If a story is not for you, then you can ignore it. If you don't like what a particular journalist is writing on social media, you can always unfollow or mute them.

I actually know and work with a few people who don't like transfers and I totally understand and respect them. At the same time, I have a job to do and I will always try and do it to the very best of my ability. If some people – and I'm including journalists as well as fans in this – don't like transfers that's absolutely fine. The good news for them is that they probably won't be reading this book anyway.

In the media, we all have different jobs to do and one of my jobs is to report on transfers. Other people have different jobs to do in sports journalism and they do them very well. There are brilliant, dogged investigative reporters who uncover all sorts of things that people don't want us to know; there are journalists who write beautifully about games they are at; there are other journalists who write fascinating interviews, features and hard–hitting columns. I guess what I am trying to say is that there is something for everyone and everyone is free to like what they like and ignore what they don't like.

Football has never been covered in so much detail on so many platforms and I am just a very small voice in a very crowded space. Some people absolutely love transfers and they spend the two windows every year reading and watching and listening to everything they can get their hands on about the twists and turns of all the deals that are being discussed.

Some people don't like how huge the coverage of transfers has become, especially on social media, and I can appreciate how they feel.

What I would say in my defence is that there is an insatiable appetite for transfer news and sometimes stories are so big that they have to be covered every day. They are so big that my colleagues and I are trying to get inside information and updates on them every day.

I know transfers are not for everybody, but they are for a lot of people. I am in the lucky position that I often get stopped on the street by football fans who want to talk to me. I promise you the number one topic of conversation is usually about transfers. People want to know who their club are buying, they want the latest information on particular transfers. I have to admit, sometimes the people who stop me on the street know more about football than I do, especially the youngsters. It always astonishes me how much these boys and girls know about the game now. I suppose it is because they have access to so much information, statistics, data and videos on their phones and tablets. When I was a kid, we had to make do with a copy of my father's paper and a comic or a packet of stickers if we had been well behaved.

I have to admit that sometimes when I am stopped on the street and asked about transfers, I can actually tell people more face-to-face than I can report on the TV, radio or social media. When you are broadcasting live or putting something out on social media, you have to be smart about your phrasing. For a start, you don't want to reveal your sources or upset them, and you don't want to upset the player involved or the clubs or, just as importantly, the fans.

For instance, I have some good friends who are Tottenham fans and they used to get upset about the number of stories there were linking Harry Kane with other clubs. Whenever there was a transfer story about Kane, at least one of them would message me to complain about how unfair it was that the media were talking about Kane when there really wasn't a story there at all. If it was from a reputable source, I knew that there was something in the story, but at the same time I could understand why it was frustrating for Tottenham supporters to constantly see their main man being linked with other clubs. Fans have every right to be passionate about their clubs and to defend the interests of their clubs, so we have to be very careful with the words we choose to use when we are talking about transfers and, of course, as always we have to make sure everything we are saying is based on facts.

When it comes to moves that do not work out for whatever reason I also try and choose my words carefully. It's not for me to say that someone has been a bad buy or a total waste of money. I can comment on an individual performance if I watched a player play live in a game but the rest of the time I prefer to leave the judgements and the opinions to the experts or the fans. I'm just a reporter, my job is not to judge players, there are plenty of former players and managers in the media who are in a much better and more informed position than me to talk about a particular player's perceived

Hanging up the yellow tie – which now lives in the National Football Museum in Manchester! *(© Vishal Sharma 2013)*

Trying to get a word with the legend Brian Clough when his Forest side met Celtic in the early eighties.
(© National World Newsprints, Donald Macleod)

With Nicola Cortese and Mauricio Pochettino, then both of Southampton FC! *(© Jim White)*

News coming in during another Deadline Day, this time alongside former Sky presenter Natalie Sawyer.
(© Katie Anderson)

Meeting Medhi Benatia in Munich, after the famed tweet that he was on his way to Manchester United. *(© Katie Anderson)*

On the day I met Farhad Moshiri, 2016.
(© Jim White)

No Deadline Day was complete without Harry Redknapp!

Interviewing the late, great David Bowie in 1983! (© STV)

Sir Alex . . . the best.
(© Gerardo Jaconelli)

Fun on set at Sky with Kate Abdo.
(© Katie Anderson)

The yellow tie – a must-wear on Deadline Day at Sky!
(© Katie Anderson)

Draped the yellow tie on the then Chelsea manager José Mourinho who thanked me – then gave it back! (© *Sky Sports*)

With then Patriots star quarterback Tom Brady and now Birmingham City investor! (© *Katie Anderson*)

The quite wonderful late Ray Wilkins who gave me an interview and bailed me out! *(© Jim White)*

Love an interview with Noel – Manchester City super fan! *(© Katie Anderson)*

Big names who all had big career moves – Ronaldinho, Sergio Ramos and the Brazilian Ronaldo! *(© Katie Anderson)*

Graeme Souness – a huge help to me during my career. *(© Jim White)*

On set as the window slams shut! *(© Sky Sports)*

On Deadline Day set with Harry! *(© Jim White)*

Gareth Bale to Real Madrid update! *(© Sky Sports)*

A bizarrely memorable trip to Cardiff City owner Vincent Tan's yacht in the South China Sea. *(© Jim White)*

Peter Odemwingie's Deadline Day story remains one of the most intriguing to this day! *(© Jim White)*

Covering the 1989 World Youth Tournament in Glasgow, with legendary Pelé and the late Ian St John.

Me in Genoa doing the Souness STV documentary back when he played for Sampdoria, 1985. *(© STV)*

Fraser Robertson
1971-2019

Fraser Robertson, to whom the book is dedicated. *(© Sky Sports)*

shortcomings. I think it's fine to praise players, but criticising them is a line I try not to cross. I'm more than happy to talk about what great buys Erling Haaland or Kieran Trippier, for example, have proved to be, but I would rather not get involved in any personal criticism.

I was at the London Stadium in May 2023 when the Manchester United goalkeeper, David De Gea, made a bad mistake to allow West Ham United to score the only goal of the game. De Gea was in the spotlight again for all the wrong reasons because it was the sixth mistake he had made that season which had led to the opposition scoring a goal. When you are a goalkeeper, you have to get used to scrutiny – there is nowhere to hide if you make a mistake. If you are United's keeper, millions of people around the world are going to be watching you even more closely and analysing, debating and judging everything you do during a game. The spotlight can be an unforgiving place, especially with the free-for-all nature of modern social media, and that is why I have so much respect for professional footballers, and especially goalkeepers.

The mistake – letting a pretty soft long-range Saïd Benrahma strike beat him despite getting a hand to the ball – could not have come at a worse time for De Gea, because he was in the middle of contract renewal talks with United. Now, everyone seems to have an opinion on whether De Gea is good enough to be United's goalkeeper. He has been at Old Trafford since 2011 and, despite making many crucial saves and keeping more clean sheets than any other United goalkeeper, there have been a growing number of detractors who are convinced that he should not be the first-choice goalkeeper at a top Premier League club with title-winning aspirations.

Modern goalkeepers have to be comfortable with the ball at their feet and they have to be able to play out from the back, like Álisson at Liverpool or Ederson at Manchester City. Most teams these days like to control possession and the goalkeeper has to be almost as good an outfield player as the other players in the team. De Gea has historically been a very good shot-stopper, but the general consensus appears to be that playing football with his feet is not the strongest part of his game.

I was at the London Stadium, I saw De Gea's mistake with my own eyes and I spoke to some of the players and coaches about it after the game. Despite all that, I still didn't feel like I was in a position to criticise De Gea on my radio show over the following days when his contract situation and future at United became a big talking point. Don't get me wrong, of course I have an opinion about it, but at the end of the day my opinion doesn't really matter and people don't listen to my radio show to hear my opinions.

I have two jobs. I am a reporter and a presenter. My job is to get stories and interviews and also to present my show in an engaging and informative way – and to do my best to get the opinions of the experts. Now, the experts can be former players and managers and owners and referees or anyone else involved in the game, but they can also be supporters, especially the ones who go to every game and see everything with their own eyes.

A few days after De Gea's mistake against West Ham, I was doing my show with Simon Jordan and Danny Murphy. They both had strong opinions about De Gea and that's absolutely fine because they both know what they are talking about. Danny is an astute observer of the game and he played with some brilliant goalkeepers during his career. Simon also knows the game inside out from the boardroom perspective and he was more than qualified to talk about De Gea, and especially his contract situation, because Simon had bought and sold goalkeepers himself and been involved in contract negotiations with them.

When you have experts like Danny and Simon in the studio, why would anyone want to know what yours truly thinks about De Gea? We had a very good debate on the show and, as I could see that Danny and Simon both had doubts about him, I tried to test their arguments by presenting the other side of the story, by highlighting all the great saves De Gea had made, all the games which he had won almost single-handedly for United, and his amazing clean sheet record. Of course, I could have said what perhaps I really thought – that it was another shocking mistake and it was no wonder De Gea couldn't get into the Spain squad any more. I could have pointed out that he hadn't played for his country since 2020. I think I would have been letting myself and my listeners down if I had done that. I'm always looking for balance and informed opinion on my show. I don't want a shouting match or a pile-on.

As it turned out United let De Gea leave when his contract ran out in July 2023. He became a free agent after twelve years at Old Trafford and United paid Inter Milan £55 million for André Onana to become their new number one.

Although a lot of people seem to associate me with transfers, there are other aspects of being a sports journalist which can be much more rewarding than breaking a transfer story. I always plan my radio shows in advance and, one morning in May 2023, I noticed that West Ham United were playing AZ Alkmaar in the first leg of a Europa Conference League semi-final at the London Stadium. I had been to watch West Ham beat Manchester United a few days earlier and had managed to interview their manager David Moyes and captain Declan Rice after the game. Those interviews had been mostly about United. Moyes and a player, Jarrod Bowen, would be speaking to the media the day before the AZ game.

I needed something different, something that other outlets were not going to have, something that would give my listeners a different perspective about what to expect from the game. It was while I was doing my research on AZ that I remembered that one of their former managers was Dick Advocaat. I had got to know Advocaat when he managed Rangers between 1998 and 2001, and when I contacted him he said he would be happy to come on my show to talk about AZ. What made the interview even more informative was the fact that Advocaat was the manager of ADO Den Haag in the Netherlands and, although they played in the division below AZ, he could still tell us a lot about how they played and what West Ham should expect when they faced them over two legs in their European semi-final.

I had kept in touch with Advocaat even though he had only had one job in Britain – seventeen games as Sunderland manager in 2015 – since he left Ibrox in 2001. You can certainly say he was well-travelled because, since leaving Rangers, he had nineteen different jobs in twenty-one years in ten different countries.

If you only use your contacts to try and get transfer stories, you are not doing your job properly and your contacts will see right through you. When you get to know someone who is so knowledgeable and has experienced so many different football cultures, there is a lot more to talk about than transfers. Of course, if there is a deal I think Advocaat may be involved in then there is no reason why I wouldn't contact him to see if I could find anything out about it. The rest of the time, I am always here for him if he needs to know anything about what is happening in English and Scottish football and I know he will do his best to help me out if I need anything from him.

Looking back, I still have amazing memories of how I first got to know Advocaat. In the spring of 1998, Rangers announced that he would be taking over as manager when Walter Smith stepped down in the summer. When Rangers announced that Advocaat was taking over, they made it clear that he was not going to speak about his new job until the current season had ended out of respect for PSV Eindhoven who he was managing at the time. Well, that was the proverbial red rag to a bull as far as I was concerned. I remember thinking to myself, I am going to Eindhoven and I am going to get him.

The first thing I needed to do was to get a phone number for Advocaat and, after a few calls, I had what I needed. I called him as soon as I got his number and luckily he was home but he didn't seem too thrilled to be called at home by a young – at the time – TV reporter from Glasgow. When I asked him if I could come to Eindhoven to interview him he said 'no' about five times, but in my usual style I didn't take that as him totally ruling it out. As far as I was concerned, five rejections could still become a yes. I thought his refusal to agree to an interview was his opening gambit in a game which could still end with me getting what I wanted. That's why I didn't give up and that's why I kept asking him the same question about an interview in slightly different ways, until we came to a very ad hoc arrangement with him saying that I was welcome to travel all the way to the Netherlands. But he said he couldn't promise anything and the possibility of speaking to me on camera would depend on a lot of things out of his control.

That was good enough for me and before he could change his mind I was in a travel agency in Glasgow booking a return flight to Amsterdam. Once I landed there a few days later, I met up with a local cameraman and we made our way to Den Bosch, where the local team were playing Advocaat's PSV Eindhoven in a Dutch Cup game. From

what I can remember, PSV were the overwhelming favourites, especially because they had quality players like Jaap
Stam, Phillip Cocu and Arthur Numan in their starting
eleven.

Before the game, I managed to get close enough to
introduce myself to Advocaat and I asked him if we could
grab a word with him after the match. I think he was
impressed with the fact that I followed through on what
I'd said I was going to do by travelling all the way to the
game just on the off chance that he would agree to talk to
me – even though PSV and Rangers had both insisted that
he would not be talking about his move to Ibrox until the
end of the season. Although I could sense he was impressed
with my persistence and perseverance, that was not going
to be enough to get me the interview I so desperately
wanted. Advocaat said we might be able to talk after the
game as long as PSV won. 'If we lose,' he said, 'no talk.'

I was happy with that arrangement because I didn't have a
choice. PSV were the favourites and I couldn't see how they
were going to lose, especially after they took the lead in the
sixteenth minute through a goal by their Danish forward,
Peter Møller. Everything seemed to be going according to
plan and I was relaxing in the stands, thinking about what I
was going to ask Advocaat when, about midway through the
second half, the unthinkable happened and Den Bosch
equalised.

The game finished 1–1 after 90 minutes and so it went
into extra time, because this was a knockout game and there

had to be a winner on the night. To say I was a bag of nerves at this stage would be an understatement. I panicked every time Den Bosch attacked, as I pictured myself travelling back to Glasgow with nothing to show for my efforts except a Den Bosch v PSV Eindhoven match programme. Advocaat's words kept ringing in my ears as the game restarted – 'If we lose, no talk' – and my nerves were in an even worse state when the cameraman told me the next goal would be a golden goal. As soon as somebody scored in extra time the game would end and they would be the winners. If there was no goal, the game would go to penalties. Not many people would describe Den Bosch v PSV Eindhoven some twenty-five years ago in the round of 16 of the Dutch Cup as one of the most memorable games of their lives, but it is right up there for me.

With four minutes left of the first half of extra time, PSV Eindhoven's Brazilian substitute Cláudio scored the golden goal and I am not too ashamed to say I was almost on the pitch alongside him trying to put the ball in the back of the net. I can't be sure, but I think the cameraman had to stop me running on the pitch to celebrate the goal and the dramatic win with Cláudio and his teammates.

I cannot put into words how relieved I was when that goal went in and the game ended straight away. I raced around to the dugout, where I managed to grab hold of Advocaat and convince him to let me interview him there and then on the side of the pitch. I had to start off by asking him a few questions about the game but he knew I was there to talk about Rangers and he was good enough to answer my questions about his new job in the summer.

I kept the tape of the interview very close to me as I made my way back home and I was on cloud nine all the way back to Glasgow. Despite all the obstacles that had been put in my way, I had managed to get what I, and Rangers supporters all around the world, wanted – the first interview with the new manager.

By the way, I still refuse to take no for an answer when it comes to interviewing new managers. Clubs always want to keep their managers quiet until they are unveiled at an official press conference but I always want to get my own interview as soon as possible. My radio show is on from 10 a.m. to 1 p.m. every weekday, so you also have to keep in mind that any press conferences that start after my show has finished are no good to me.

At the beginning of May 2023, Leeds United were in relegation trouble and as a last throw of the dice they sacked Javi Gracia and replaced him with Sam Allardyce. Leeds said that Allardyce would be speaking to the media in the afternoon, after his appointment had been officially announced. That would be no good to me because my show would be finished by then. I've known Allardyce for a long time, so I called him early in the morning and asked if he would give me, my listeners and Leeds fans a few words about the big challenge he was taking on at Elland Road. Although this was hours before his official press conference, Allardyce was happy to speak. I am pleased to say he is the kind of man who has enough confidence in himself to speak to whoever he wants to speak to whenever he wants to speak to them.

Men like Allardyce and Advocaat are from a generation when managers mixed more freely with journalists and they are far less likely to do just what they are told to do at all times by the media departments of their clubs. I will never forget how Advocaat helped me out that night in Den Bosch and I think he still remembers it as well. Soon after that interview, I was offered a job by Sky and, to this day, he jokes that he was the one who got me the job by giving me that interview.

By the way, Advocaat was a fantastic guest when we had him on to talk about the challenge West Ham faced against AZ. 'The Little General' is a great authority on the game and when he speaks, you listen. He knew everything there was to know about AZ and he said they would be good technically but would struggle to match West Ham's physicality and fitness in the latter stages of the game. That evening the game panned out as Advocaat had predicted. AZ looked like a good side and they took the lead in the first half, but West Ham came back after the break and scored twice to win the game 2–1.

We had Gordon Strachan on the show that May morning as well and he is someone I have known for even longer than Advocaat. I think I first saw Strachan when he was playing for Dundee against Rangers on 29 November 1975. My father had taken me to Ibrox and a little eighteen-year-old Dundee midfielder with ginger hair really caught my eye and captured my imagination – even though Rangers won the game 2–1.

I hadn't asked Strachan on to the show to talk about his Dundee days though; the reason I had invited him on was because that very day, 11 May 2023, was the fortieth anniversary of Aberdeen's incredible 2–1 win over Real Madrid in the final of the European Cup Winners' Cup in Gothenburg. Strachan played in that famous game, although as we found out during the interview, he didn't remember much about it and it had taken him more than thirty years to get around to watching it back on TV for the first time.

Although Strachan may not have remembered much about the actual game, he remembered the occasion. Like a lot of footballers, he doesn't remember every kick of every game but he does remember the emotions associated with the game, the highs and the lows, the good times and the bad.

Beating Real Madrid in a European final was the best of times and Strachan told a great story about how he had gone out to warm up on the pitch before the game. It was raining non-stop, and in those days he had long hair that was wet and getting in his eyes. There was only one thing for it – when he was back in the dressing room, he asked the physio for some scissors and he proceeded to give himself an impromptu haircut there and then. It is difficult to imagine something like that happening these days but then I suppose it is difficult to imagine Aberdeen beating the mighty Real Madrid these days as well.

Some journalists have found Strachan a little bit difficult to handle and he is definitely someone who likes doing things his own way. Having said that, he has a wonderfully dry sense of humour, he is great company and no one can argue with his record as a player and manager. I think some of the assumptions about his tricky relationship with journalists come from a famous encounter with a reporter when he was manager of Southampton. After a game, a TV reporter approached Strachan and asked him for a quick word. Strachan said 'Velocity' and walked off.

That is typical of Gordon Strachan, his dry sense of humour and his quick – or should I say velocity? – thinking. It was eleven years after I first saw Strachan play that I got to know him a little bit when he played for Scotland at the World Cup in 1986. I remember him being very friendly and helpful and that is exactly the way I found him some ten years later when he was managing Coventry City and I went to interview him in his office. This was in the days before everyone had laptops and iPads and mobile phones, and halfway through our chat the fax machine in the corner of his office burst into life. Strachan went over to see what was coming out of it. 'Look at this, Jim,' he said. 'It's an agent offering me a player called Luís Figo.'

Chapter 8

The Media is the Message

Many of the changes in the way transfers are reported have been brought about by the incredible growth of social media. Nearly every football reporter in the world uses it now. Martin Samuel of *The Times* seems to be about one of the only journalists left who wants nothing to do with it. Everybody else seems to be on it.

There's an interesting debate about whether journalists should even put their stories on social media because the social media companies don't pay us a penny. Are the social media companies exploiting our vanity by expecting us to provide them with a constant stream of stories for nothing in return except likes, retweets and followers?

I am a late convert because I only joined Twitter in December 2013. People from Twitter had actually been in touch with me before to ask me to join, but I wasn't really sure it was for me. I finally took the plunge after a charity event at Old Trafford with Sir Alex Ferguson and Darren Fletcher. By the way, Sir Alex had nothing to do with my decision. I am sure if I had asked him for his advice he would have told me to have nothing to do with it.

I'm still very cautious about using social media and I am by no means what you would call a prolific tweeter. I am still old-fashioned in the way that my first loyalty is to my listeners and viewers. If I have a story or an update, I will put it out on my talkSPORT radio show first. When you are presenting a three-hour live show every weekday you don't really have time to share your every mundane thought or opinion with the rest of the world on social media.

Posting on social media can be an unnerving experience. I always feel apprehensive just before I tweet something. I read my tweets over and over again just to make sure that they say exactly what I mean because there's always a real danger that people will misunderstand what you are trying to say.

I have to admit I use social media less and less for transfer stories these days. There are some great transfer reporters on social media and they are the new breed, the younger generation who have grown up in the age of the smartphone and the internet. They provide an invaluable service but I like to think there's still space in the transfer ecosystem for what some people would call old-fashioned reporters who still go to games and press conferences and talk to people and meet people and build up their contacts.

I like to meet people and build relationships rather than just message them back and forth all day, every day. The ideal position to be in is to have contacts at all the big clubs and with all the high-profile players, managers and agents.

I am not criticising the reporters who work only on social

media and online because some of them do a fantastic job, especially the ones who have great contacts outside the UK. The most famous transfer reporter on social media is the phenomenon that is Fabrizio Romano. He operates at an incredibly high level and the size of his following is testimony to his reliability. I have had him as a guest on my radio show and he always delivers, whether it's on a big breaking transfer story or updating a developing story. He has become the amazon.com of transfers and he seems to be across every story. The only danger with having such a massive following on social media, though, is that the work of other reporters can sometimes get overlooked.

Social media and football are not always a good mix and I have a lot of sympathy for people who are abused, belittled and ridiculed online. The people who are spreading all this hate often don't realise the consequences of their actions. If you are in the public eye and you are on social media, you have to have coping strategies to deal with all the hate and negativity and I have one that works perfectly. I ignore it all.

I am being totally honest. As soon as I see one abusive message I just close down the app on my phone and I go and do something else instead. I don't take it personally because I hardly see any of it and I honestly don't care. The people who are spreading this hate don't know me, so why would I be affected by what they say or think? It would be different if my friends or colleagues were on Twitter slagging me off but – to the best of my knowledge – that hasn't happened yet.

Having said all that, I don't want to be too negative about social media because it can be a very positive and effective tool. One area of my life where I think it has made a real difference is my sobriety. I have made no secret of the fact that I used to have a drink problem. I used to drink far too much, usually Guinness, then whisky and then all the problems would start.

I stopped drinking in 2011 but I should have stopped years before that. In 1999, Graeme Souness was managing Benfica and I went to Portugal to interview him. I had known him for something like thirteen years by then and we got on well. We were close enough for him to care about my health and wellbeing and that must be why he took me to one side and told me that I needed to stop drinking. I should have listened to him. It would have made a real difference to my life and the lives of lots of other people if I had listened, but I carried on drinking and drinking until I couldn't drink any more.

I stopped drinking on 28 October 2011. You might already know that if you follow me on social media. I post a message and a picture of myself every year on that date. It's just a way to mark another year being sober and to encourage and help anyone else who might be in the same position I was. The response to those pictures is incredible and it has also allowed me to connect privately with a few people who are going through what I went through.

So social media is not all doom and gloom – it can help you to help others and of course it can drum up interest in what you are up to if you are in the public eye. In October 2018, I managed to set up an exclusive interview with the Belgian businessman Roland Duchâtelet, who owned Charlton Athletic at the time. He was a very controversial character and Charlton fans were campaigning to get him out of their club. He wasn't going to games any more because of fears about his safety.

I was told if I went to Brussels he would talk to me, so we arranged a time and date and he gave me the address of a hotel where he would meet me. You are always worried that the person you have arranged to interview will change their mind at the last minute and until they actually appear you can't be totally sure that the interview is going to happen.

Thankfully, Duchâtelet turned up on that Saturday morning and the interview lasted for about forty minutes. He answered all my questions and nothing was off limits. I got on with him as well, which made him relax and speak as openly as possible. I didn't like his style of ownership but I liked him as a person.

As soon as the interview was over, I was on social media teasing the fact that we had got the interview and people could listen to it on Monday morning. Charlton fans would be very interested because he admitted to me that he might sell the club.

As it was the weekend, I didn't have to go back to London straight away, so I stayed in the hotel for a few more hours and had lunch with Duchâtelet. In contrast to their public personas, nearly everyone you meet in football is open and friendly in private and Duchâtelet was no different. The interview had been all about him and what he thought, whereas lunch seemed to be all about me. He wanted to know about me and my career and he also wanted to know all about Brexit.

I'm not sure I was the best person to talk about that but I was more than happy to tell him what I thought and he seemed quite interested in what I had to say. Anyway, the only reason I am mentioning my interview with Duchâtelet is to show how useful social media can be to signpost projects that you are working on and let as many people as possible know about them in advance.

Of course, you have to strike the right balance and you should only post about things which you think your followers will be interested in. I knew that a lot of my followers would be interested in an exclusive interview with one of the most controversial owners in English football. A picture of what I had to eat at the lunch or what I was wearing? Not so much.

By the way, in case you are wondering, I did pay for the lunch and very nice it was too. But being serious, sometimes it can be dangerous to give too much away on social media. For instance, advertising the fact that you've got a big interview before it airs could alert other people to try and get their own interview, but in this case I wasn't worried about that at all. I knew no one else was going to get what I had. I am always confident in my own abilities – without that confidence and inner belief you are never going to get anywhere in this business. Though it's always healthy to have some doubts, because you don't want to end up being too full of yourself. It's only natural to worry that someone else is going to get a story before you or that someone will change their mind and not turn up for an interview. Don't worry, I know all about getting stood up – going all the way back to my student days in Edinburgh.

In those days, there was no social media or apps to help you meet members of the opposite sex. You had to rely on your own charm – although I'm not sure I had any – and a bit of confidence fuelled by alcohol. I guess that's where my problem with drink started and it got me into plenty of scrapes during my career before I finally kicked the habit and cleaned myself up totally once and for all.

One of my worst experiences was in 1987 when Ray Wilkins came to Glasgow to sign for Rangers from Paris Saint-Germain. I had been tipped off about the flight he was going to be on, so I arranged to meet my STV cameraman at Glasgow airport in order to get an exclusive interview with Ray as he flew in to sign for his new club.

The only problem was I had had a few drinks and I missed Ray. There was no way I could go back to the office without the interview, so I had to come up with a Plan B. Luckily Ibrox is not far away from the airport, so we got there as quickly as possible and I somehow managed to convince Ray to come out and let us film him walking back into the stadium as if he had just arrived. He also let me interview him. He knew I had messed up and he helped me out. He got me out of a very big hole and I never forgot that.

From then on, we always stayed in touch and I am proud to say that I knew him. He was an absolute gentleman. He was fascinating company and he was a great storyteller. People sometimes forget what a brilliant player he was. Imagine being Chelsea captain when you are just seventeen and then going on to play for clubs like Manchester United and AC Milan as well as your country.

I was shattered when Ray died in 2018. The great and the good were at his funeral and that just showed the kind of man he was. I always post something on social media on the anniversary of his passing. I do it to commemorate him and to keep him in our thoughts, and every year there is a great reaction.

The day after Ray died we paid tribute to him as best as we could on my show and we had one amazing call out of the blue which stopped everyone in their tracks. I think the clip has had almost six million views on social media now, but I didn't know what to expect when we put someone on live who wanted to talk about Ray. This is what he said:

'I'm an ex-soldier and I had some time where I was homeless. I was outside Brompton station and he came over to me and I recognised him straight away. He just took some time to sit and chat, and we were both sat on my piece of cardboard together. We were chatting about the army. I was a gambler at the time – I'm still a gambler but I am recovering – and he took the time. He even took a phone call and he said, "Look, I'll call you back, I'm busy at the moment."

'We were sat chatting and he gave me £20 and he told me to get myself a hot meal and he took me across the road to buy me a coffee. As the bill came, I asked him, "Can I please buy this? I want to feel like a man." He said he understood all of that.

'That night, I took that £20 and got some shelter and I had a hot meal. During that time, when I was in the shelter, I met a guy who was helping ex-soldiers who put me in touch with decent people who would help me. I'm now fully recovered, not gambling, I have my own place, a beautiful girlfriend who I am about to marry and I put it down to the time that man took to give to a man that was nothing to him, a stranger, and I'm sorry if I'm getting emotional but he was a real, real hero to me and to millions of others across the world. Thank you for giving me the time to say thank you to a man I never got to say thank you to, not really. Anyone who phones in today with a memory of Ray is basically saying to his family: "Thank you for giving us Ray Wilkins."'

The fact that clip has been listened to so many times shows you how much good social media can do, but unfortunately we seem to live in a world where too many people are encouraged to rush to judgement and write or say whatever is in their head. Social media companies make a lot of money from people arguing on their platforms. Their business models are based on algorithms which direct you towards topics which are trending and which they think, based on your past use of the platform, you will be interested in.

I've already mentioned that I was at the West Ham v Manchester United game in May 2023 when David De Gea made a terrible mistake. Within seconds, he was trending on Twitter for all the wrong reasons and people were kicking him when he was down. Bad news is good news for social media. The ultimate aim of platforms is to engage you for as long as possible, they want to rile up your emotions and get you to take part in the hot topic of the day, hour or minute. The longer you spend on their platforms, the more money they can make from advertising.

It's a ruthless and very effective business model. At the same time, it can do a lot of harm, not just to the people who are being mocked and criticised but also to the people who are using the platforms every day, the people whose emotions can be manipulated for profit. Don't get me wrong, I use social media and it makes my job easier in a lot of ways. Having said that, I'm also aware of how dangerous and damaging it can be for society and for everyone's mental health.

It can be especially damaging for professional footballers who do their jobs in the unforgiving glare of the public eye. It's something modern players have to deal with and I know some of them have to get professional help to cope. I don't know Jason Steele personally, but the Brighton goalkeeper spoke to the media at the end of the 2022–23 season and what he said really put the problem into focus for me. He is one of many players who have stepped away from social media and closed their accounts because of the amount of negativity and criticism. What people tend to forget is the effect the abuse has – not just on the player, but also on their families. We are all human and it affected Steele so much that he ended up hating football. Luckily he put that all behind him when he moved to Brighton and he produced some outstanding performances when he got more chances to play in the first team under Roberto De Zerbi.

When you are a player you will be targeted for abuse even if you don't have any social media accounts. The abuse comes from people reacting to your performances and any stories that may be out there about you. For journalists, the abuse will be triggered by what you write or say and, as a result, people are becoming much more guarded when it comes to expressing themselves.

Personally speaking, I'm not sure the keyboard warriors are the reason why, more often than not, I like to keep my opinions to myself. I think it has more to do with the fact that I was taught as a trainee journalist and throughout my career that I should be as objective as possible. I don't want to sound too precious here because, at the end of the day, I know football is just a game and there are far more important things going on around the world every second of every day. I think perspective is very important in life and in journalism and I think social media is encouraging us to lose our sense of it by tempting us to say the first thing that comes into our heads all the time.

One of the most serious and pernicious aspects of football and its relationship with social media is the racist abuse of players on platforms like Twitter and Instagram. I was once sent to Twitter's head office in central London to see if I could get anyone there to talk to me after yet another player had been racially abused on their platform. Paul Pogba had missed a penalty in a live TV game for Manchester United against Wolves in August 2019 and the neanderthals had been out on social media again.

When something like that happens – unfortunately far too regularly these days – journalists usually contact the social media company in question. All they get is a bland and pretty meaningless statement which says that they are taking the issue seriously but doesn't actually amount to very much at all. People in the game are sick of the racism on social media and they want something done about it – not just words on yet another press release.

In my experience, the social media companies are also reluctant to address the problem in public. Journalists keep asking them to come out and speak to us in front of a camera and microphone about the problem and what they are doing about it, but they refuse to engage, preferring instead to issue faceless press releases by email.

There was something about what happened to Pogba which made me think that I wanted answers from the social media companies. A statement released to the press wasn't going to be enough for me this time. I live close to central London so it didn't take me long to jump on the underground to the station closest to Twitter's office in the capital. Despite it being right bang in the centre of London, in one of the busiest areas of town, full of shoppers and tourists and office workers, it wasn't easy to find Twitter's UK headquarters.

There was not a single sign or logo on the building. Nothing to suggest at all that this was the London home of one of the biggest social media companies in the world. Twitter had released a standard response to requests from journalists about the abuse directed at Pogba on their platform. They said that Twitter 'takes action against behaviour that targets individuals with hateful conduct.' That wasn't good enough for me and it wasn't good enough for a lot of people in football. Yet again, a player was being racially abused on social media and the platform in question didn't seem to be doing enough to stop it from happening again and again.

Not for the first, or, unfortunately, the last time, Pogba's teammates and fellow professionals took to social media themselves to express their disgust and demand meaningful action. United defender Harry Maguire summed up the way many footballers were feeling when he posted this on Twitter:

'Disgusting. Social media need to do something about it . . . Every account that is opened should be verified by a passport/driving licence. Stop these pathetic trolls making numerous accounts to abuse people. @Twitter @instagram'

I spent a few hours that morning outside Twitter's offices trying to find people who worked there who would be willing to talk to me. Nobody wanted to speak. I would have liked to ask them what it felt like to work for a company which provided a platform for people to post that kind of filth. I have faith in human nature so I am sure a lot of them were concerned but no one wanted to speak.

The Alan Turing Institute produced a report tracking the abuse of footballers on Twitter during the first five months of the 2021–22 Premier League season. They analysed more than 2.3 million tweets and what they found shows the scale of the problem. The good news is that they found that 55 per cent of tweets about players were positive and 27 per cent were neutral. That's where the good news ends. When it comes to the remaining 16 per cent of the tweets, 12.5 per cent were critical, 3.5 per cent were abusive and 8.6 per cent of the abusive tweets contained a reference to the player's identity, for example his race, religion, gender or sexuality. The report says there were 5,148 of these discriminatory abusive tweets during the first five months of that season.

The report is a very sobering read and I have to say I was shocked to discover that one in fourteen players receive abuse every day. Now imagine the effect that can have on somebody. A lot of the time, if I feel like I am being abused on Twitter, I can stop tweeting and the problem will slowly start to go away. High-profile players don't really have that option because they are not being abused for anything they have posted on social media, they are being abused for just doing their job and their job is always in the public eye.

Hundreds of abusive tweets are being sent every day and the problem affects about 70 per cent of Premier League players. Many of the victims are from minority ethnic backgrounds. According to the report, a lot of these attacks take place during 'footballing flashpoints, including high-profile transfers or a loss on the pitch.'

Lots of reports are produced about lots of different issues and it is easy to be cynical about them and ignore their findings. Sometimes, though, the things they find out really stop you in your tracks and make you think. What sort of game has football become if players are being racially abused just because they may be at the centre of a transfer story? What sort of society are we living in when people think they can just pick up their phones during games and start typing out racist messages about players?

Before reading the report, I had assumed that the main triggers for this kind of abuse were flashpoints during games. For instance, when someone misses an easy chance or a penalty, or someone scores an own goal, and before you know it the player is trending on Twitter and everyone is kicking him when he is down. While I've always known that there is a huge amount of interest about transfers, I hadn't realised how many people would take them so seriously that they would see it as an invitation, and use it as an excuse, to abuse players.

In my opinion, the rise of this kind of abuse and the failure to stop it is one of the worst things about the modern game. When I am presenting my radio show, my bosses and I are responsible for what goes out on air and we are regulated by Ofcom. I find it difficult to believe that any platform is allowed to publish the kinds of things you see on social media. I also find it difficult to believe that the people who work at these companies tolerate what they are facilitating and amplifying. That's why I went to Twitter's offices myself the morning after Pogba was abused for missing a penalty.

I know quite a few journalists who have mixed emotions about putting their stories on social media, and not just because of all the hate and abuse which seems to proliferate on the platforms. Starting out as a journalist, I was very aware that I worked for my employer and they paid me and my wages paid my bills. Social media doesn't pay journalists. They get all their content free. In theory it should be a quid pro quo. The platform gets content without having to pay for it and the journalist gets exposure for his work and his employer and a higher profile. That is the way that it should work, but because of the free-for-all some of the platforms have become, a lot of my colleagues are beginning to think they should cut back on using social media.

If you are writing in a newspaper, or talking on radio or TV, you have time and space to say what you have to say. On Twitter, the character limit means that the few sentences you have written can easily be taken out of context or people can misunderstand or misrepresent what you are trying to say. Writing in a newspaper, or speaking on TV and radio, is like having a telephone conversation with someone, whereas social media is like sending them a text message.

When it comes to transfers, you have to be very careful to make sure you are not going to offend anyone before you tweet something. The best way to do that is to stick to facts and leave the opinions to the experts. For instance, I remember lots of discussion and debate in January 2023 about why Manchester United had decided to sign Wout Weghorst on loan from Burnley. Everyone knew United needed a striker but most people were expecting them to spend money on someone, not take a player on loan from a Championship club who had loaned him out to a Turkish team.

I think there were legitimate questions to ask about the thinking behind the deal, but it wouldn't have been right for me to make disparaging remarks about the signing. What was interesting for me was *why* United had signed Weghorst. Was it because he was really the player Erik ten Hag wanted or was the manager operating with one hand tied behind his back? Was there no money in January because United had spent so much in the summer of 2022, and the club had effectively been put up for sale by its owners, the Glazer family, in November of the same year?

I think that is a very legitimate question and, as a presenter, it is exactly the kind of question I ask the experts on my shows. I'm not sure anyone needs to know what I think about it though, and if I was to tweet my thoughts I could end up being in the middle of an argument with people I don't know. If a United fan was to stop me in the street and ask me that question I would happily stop and chat about it. I just think getting involved in arguments on social media can be very counter-productive and people often end up misunderstanding each other.

It's not just opinions that you have to be careful about expressing on social media if you are a football reporter, you also have to choose your words very carefully when it comes to protecting your sources. A lot of the time it means not revealing everything you know, at other times it means having to stay silent when people doubt the quality of your information.

Imagine an agent you know and trust has told you that a Premier League club have contacted him about a player he represents and they are willing to pay £50 million for him. After you have checked the information out with your club contacts and are sure it's true, you have to find a form of words to report it without revealing the identity of your source or anyone else you have spoken to.

Once you put the story out there, there will probably be lots of different reactions. The fans of the two clubs involved may have different opinions about whether it is a good deal, lots of people may have an opinion on the price tag, some people may think it's a good deal, some people may think it's a waste of money and some people will probably accuse you of making it all up.

Of course, you can't say everything you know, you can't reveal where the information is coming from or who you have been speaking to. You just have to grin and bear it and trust your sources. If your sources are impeccable and people you have known for a long time, you have nothing to worry about it. If your source is someone in the pub or on Twitter, you might be in trouble.

Next time you are listening to a reporter talk about a transfer, it is always worth remembering that frequently the whole truth cannot be revealed. That is just as frustrating for the reporter as it is for the people who are reading or listening or watching what has been written or said.

In that respect, it can be frustrating being a transfer reporter – a feeling managers who deal with the media during a window know only too well. You see, managers absolutely cannot reveal what they know, they have to be more than a little economical with the truth.

If you are the Manchester United manager and you are asked about a potential £50 million target during a press conference, there is very little you can say. If you are in for the player, you can't talk about it because he belongs to another club and it could jeopardise the deal in lots of different ways. If you are not in for the player, you probably don't want to say anything in public because he belongs to another club and you don't want to disrespect him or his club, nor do you want to set a precedent by talking in public about every player you have been linked with.

That's why press conferences are not the best places to get

your information from if you are looking for a transfer story. They can be very one-dimensional and all the power rests with the manager and the club. As a journalist, you are only going to get the chance to ask a couple of questions and it is very easy for you to be shut down.

If you want the real truth from a manager, you are going to have to speak to him in private. You are only going to be able to do that if you know him and he trusts you and you have his number. Even then, he may not want to tell you the whole truth because, more often than not, the deal in question will be in the balance and he will not want to jeopardise it in any way.

Some fans feel sorry for their manager and get very defensive if he is asked questions about transfers at press conferences. I don't think there is any point feeling sorry for them because they can look after themselves and, just like the reporter asking the question, they have a job to do. The question has to be asked but, ultimately, the truth is that it doesn't have to be answered totally honestly. That is why press conferences can be smoke and mirrors and you have to look and listen out for what is not revealed as much as what is said. That's only really possible if you watch a full press conference and, unless you are there, that is difficult because only clips are usually put up on social media and the internet.

By talking to the manager in private, or anyone else involved in the deal, you can get an understanding of what is happening. They may ask you not to reveal anything they are telling you and you should always respect that. But by talking to as many people as possible you can build up a picture and, when it comes to discussing the deal or writing about it, you will be in a position to do so with authority without giving away any confidential information or revealing your sources.

So press conferences can be a waste of time as a source for transfer stories but they can be exciting if a club has made a big signing and he is on stage in front of that board advertising all the club's sponsors. Back in 1998, I drove all the way from London to Middlesbrough for an audience with Paul Gascoigne. He had just moved from Rangers but I didn't go all that way because I wanted to sit in a packed room and wait my turn to ask him a question.

I went because I wanted my own interview and I backed myself to make sure that I would get what I wanted. I've known Paul for a long time and I got pretty close to him when he signed for Rangers in 1995. I got to know him then and, in those days, we were both drinkers and that could be a cocktail for disaster.

When he saw me approaching with a microphone and a cameraman, he was only too happy to stop and talk. Getting your own interview is always much better than just relying on press conferences – especially when it's with someone who is as big a star and as engaging as Paul. I'm not sure if the other journalists were happy about me getting my own interview, but you have to have a thick skin in this business and you always have to be proactive and on the front foot.

You have to make contacts, you have to gain people's trust, you can't just sit back and wait for the little morsels of information that clubs, players and managers are happy to throw your way when it suits them.

I'm still in touch with Paul and it's a measure of the man that he was one of the first people I called when I found out that Ray Wilkins had died. Some people may assume that Paul can be unreliable but that could not be further from the truth. I asked Paul if he could be on live right at the top of my radio show the next morning to talk about Ray. Paul was there on the phone ready to go at 10 a.m. and he paid a beautiful and emotional tribute to Ray.

It re-confirmed what I already knew about Paul. He has a heart of gold. Paul always went out of his way to help me when he could – even when he was in trouble. When he was at Rangers, he was late coming back from America once and the press pack were camped outside his house in Dunbartonshire. I turned up with a cameraman from STV. I went straight up to the door and rang the bell. Paul let me and the cameraman in and we were chatting away in the kitchen when the phone rang.

Paul picked it up and I could tell straight away there was something wrong. I could see the colour draining away from his face. I don't think he said a word before he handed me the phone.

'Hello, it's Jim White here. Who's that?'

'It's Walter Smith. Get out of the house now.'

I did as I was told. When the Rangers manager told you

to do something, you did it. Mind you, I did make sure that we got some nice shots of Paul, back home from America, in his own kitchen.

That encounter with Paul was long before the days of social media and I dread to think what kind of extra pressure and scrutiny players like him would have faced if things like Twitter had been around in their playing days. It doesn't take much to get people angry and riled up on social media, as I learned to my cost in the summer of 2017 when Barcelona wanted to sign Philippe Coutinho from Liverpool.

Coutinho was keen to make the move because playing for Barcelona is something that most footballers dream about when they are growing up. Coutinho had a big problem though and that problem was the fact that he had signed a new five-year Liverpool contract in January 2017. That contract didn't have a release clause, putting Liverpool in a very powerful position seven months later when Barcelona offered €100 million for Coutinho on Wednesday 9 August.

Liverpool dismissed Barcelona's offer immediately and two days later, at 10 a.m. on Friday 11 August, the club's owners, Fenway Sports Group, released a statement saying their definitive stance was that no offers for the player would be considered. That would seem to be that. Coutinho was going nowhere. Of course, not everything was as it seemed, and at midday I was told by a contact that Coutinho had handed in a transfer request.

When I reported that – and it was denied by Liverpool – it

is fair to say that a lot of people were not happy. The big questions for me were whether I would hold my nerve and if I was absolutely sure about the information. Would I stick to my story or change it because Liverpool had denied receiving a transfer request? My source had never let me down before and, after calling him again, I decided to stick with the story. The next ninety minutes were pretty uncomfortable and all I could do was hold my nerve and trust my source while lots of people seemed to be ridiculing me on social media.

Thankfully, it was confirmed at just before 2 p.m. that Coutinho had handed in a transfer request. It didn't end up doing Coutinho much good in the short term though, because Liverpool still said he was not for sale and he remained their player when the window closed at the end of the month. Coutinho had to wait until the next window to get his dream move.

Liverpool agreed to sell him to Barcelona in January for £142 million and it turned out to be a dream move – for Liverpool. They received one of the biggest transfer fees of all time and they reinvested it very wisely, buying players like Virgil van Dijk and Álisson, who helped them win the title for the first time in thirty years in 2020. Meanwhile, Coutinho struggled to justify his enormous price tag at the Nou camp, although it is often forgotten that he did win two league titles at Barcelona.

The last time I saw Coutinho was after his Aston Villa side beat Newcastle United 3–0 at Villa Park in April 2023. He wasn't in the Villa squad that day, but he was at the game with his family and I saw him looking a little bit downbeat. I didn't feel the time was right to tell him that he had been responsible for ninety of the most uncomfortable minutes of my career. Who knows, maybe looking back now, and considering how well he played when he was at Liverpool, he wishes I had been wrong all along.

Chapter 9

$1 + 1 + 1 = 111$

You can't write a book about transfers and the media without hearing from agents. The only problem is that agents, especially the ones who do most of the biggest deals, don't want to speak out too much. Some of them do give interviews from time to time but even then they don't like to give too much away.

When they do give interviews, they are generally asked about their players, particular deals or the general state of the market. They are very rarely, if ever, asked about their relationship with journalists and what they think about the way their industry is covered in the media.

For this book, in order to really get to the heart of the matter, I thought I would try a different approach. I asked some agents if they would be willing to tell me what they really think about me, my colleagues and the way we operate. I told them I didn't want them to pull any punches. I wanted their honest opinion.

I was spoiled for choice when it came to picking somebody to tell me what my industry looks like from an agent's point of view. Mark — not his real name — has been an agent for more than thirty years and he has represented some of the most famous players and clubs in the game. He's also worked on some of the biggest deals and he's still as busy as ever:

Football has changed so much over the past thirty years and that is reflected in the way the game is now covered in the media. When I started off, journalists used to get close to players and managers but that has all changed. Journalism is not what it used to be and you can't necessarily blame journalists for that. They are working in an industry that has been completely changed by the internet and social media and they are under constant pressure to get a story. As far as some of them are concerned, any story will do.

I'm in contact with a few journalists I have known for a long time and they know that when I tell them something, it is a fact. It is not second- or third-hand information that I have heard from someone who has heard it from someone else. I will only talk to them about situations I am involved in directly, but there is generally very little I can say until a deal has been signed, sealed and delivered.

The problem is that football has become so big now that supporters want to constantly know what is happening at their clubs. They want to know everything about the manager and the players and who they might be buying and selling. I feel sorry for journalists, because they are like hamsters on wheels constantly having to satisfy these demands. The problem is we live in the information age and the demand is never satisfied.

Most of the time, I don't have a particular problem with how they cover transfers. What I do sometimes have a problem with is when they are too critical too quickly about a player, manager or chairman and owners. It's very easy to criticise when you don't know exactly what's going on behind the scenes.

It goes without saying that there are also some journalists who are close to certain agents and that's why they build up players who a lot of the time are really not that special. I'm not having a go at journalists. They've got a job to do like the rest of us, it's just that it's not a job that I would want to do.

In the summer of 2022, I was dealing with one club who told me that they'd been linked with seventy-two players during the window and they hadn't signed a single one of them. I don't even know what the word linked means. Does it just mean someone else on Twitter has already written about that club's supposed interest in that player? I wouldn't be surprised.

I did end up doing a big deal for that club. I was involved in a deal that was worth £30 million and we managed to keep it under wraps until a few hours after everything had been signed. It was only then that stories started appearing saying the club were after the player. They had no idea that the deal had already been done and the player had passed his medical.

I think the coverage of transfers is pretty accurate as long as you look in the right places. If you only rely on social media, you are going to come across a lot of stuff that's just speculation and people trying to look good by pretending they're in the know. You have to be clued up and know which journalists have good contacts with a particular club. That's usually the best way of working out whether they know what they're talking about and whether they can be trusted.

A lot of the stuff that's out there is harmless, but once in a while people write something that's so wrong and potentially damaging that you have to take action. I'm not afraid of picking up the phone and having it out with a journalist when he's written something inaccurate. If it's serious and he won't back down then I've no problem getting lawyers involved. That's happened two or three times but it doesn't go that far too often. Bringing lawyers in is the last resort.

Sometimes wrong information being out there about one of your players can actually do you a favour – although even then it can be counter-productive in the long run. Usually I don't have a problem if one of my players is being linked with a move to a club like Liverpool or Man United, even if there's nothing in it. If you are going to link one of my players with Liverpool or Man United then I'm going to let you roll with it. The problems start when the player starts to believe what he reads.

From my side, it's good for his profile to be linked with big clubs, but it can come back to bite you. Give it a couple of weeks and he'll be complaining that you didn't do your job properly because you didn't get him his move to Liverpool or Real Madrid or wherever when you know they were never in for him.

I don't want to be disrespectful to certain clubs but there are a few mid-table ones you see being frequently linked with foreign players no one's ever heard of. Some journalists and the agents they're speaking to know there are Premier League clubs who are not going to kick off if their name is being used to drum up interest in a player. You see those stories a lot. There will be a list of clubs who are supposedly interested in signing the player you've never heard of and then it will say something like, 'He's valued at £20 million or £30 million.' A lot of these 'interested in' stories seem to be about foreign players because I think that they're easier to write and there's less of a chance of anyone being upset about them. If you keep writing fliers about players who already play in the Premier League, there's much more of a chance that you're going to get a call from their club or agent setting the record straight, especially if it's an English player.

They never say where this valuation comes from and few people seem to care. The journalist, if he really is one, gets what he wants and that's a story which will get him some new followers. The agent gets what he wants – the player is in the shop window. But it's not just agents doing this now. There are intermediaries trying to muscle in on deals. They might have a mandate to sell a player in one country which runs out when the window closes, so the only way they're going to make any money is if they find a buyer for the player in that country.

You've got the situation now where intermediaries are going to European clubs and getting a letter authorising them to try and sell one of their players to an English club. The clock's ticking for that intermediary. He's only going to get paid if the player is sold to an English club and he's in on the deal. That's why it's in his interest for there to be as much media interest in the player as possible. When he approaches club A to offer them the player, his hand is strengthened if they've already read about the player and think clubs B, C, D and E want to sign him.

You want to make sure you have good relationships with at least two or three journalists. It's impossible to deal with much more than that, especially during the window, and the ones I'm in touch with know that the only time I can speak to them or return their messages is early in the morning or late at night. I know that's not ideal for their deadlines but I'm too busy in the daytime during the window to be distracted by anything else except work. I've got more than five thousand contacts on my phone and I try to get back to everyone who gets in touch, but it is not always possible – especially during the summer. I don't answer any calls from unknown numbers like most people. If I get a missed call from an unknown number I'll try and message them back to find out what they want.

Journalists know how the business works and they know that you're not going to be able to spend a lot of time on the phone when you're busy. They just have to make do with the little bits of information you can give them when you can. I think people sometimes don't really understand just how complicated transfers are, especially if they involve a foreign player or foreign club. The paperwork has got even worse since Brexit, and with the amount of work that has to be done and the level of secrecy required it's impossible to give a running commentary about everything that's going on. There was one deal I was working on last summer and the complexity and the number of people and different interests involved was staggering. It almost didn't get completed because there was so much that needed to be done in a short space of time.

Negotiating the fee took ages. There was the usual song and dance about the club not wanting to sell and attempting to fine him when he went on strike to try and force through the move. The basic personal terms had already been agreed, but the problems with the fee were all to do with the structure of the payments and all the bonuses and add-ons.

Then you had to factor in all the financial fair play and tax implications in two different countries, you had to sort out the medical and have all the contracts drawn up in different languages in different countries. Don't forget that the selling club also had to factor in the sell-on clause they'd have to pay the player's previous club. They also wanted to sign a replacement player before the window closed without getting ripped off, because all the selling clubs knew that they were about to get their hands on a big pot of cash by selling your player. As well as all that, you've got the buying club now doing their best to get rid of players so they can free up spaces in their squad and stay within their wage budget.

The big issue in the deal I'm talking about was the structure of the payments. One side wanted the fee paid in five instalments over four years and the other wanted it paid in three instalments over three years. That's what it ultimately came down to and those are the details which rarely come out in the media. Usually no one involved in a deal of that size is going to want to give that kind of information away. When people don't know why a deal is taking so long, you'll see stories about 'talks are continuing' or 'a deal is getting close' or 'a deal has been agreed in principle.'

I know some agents don't like dealing with the media at all – even if they've got nothing going on. Some of them just don't like the media. A few agents don't mind having a high profile, but you only really want to be quoted by name if you're out there defending the interests of your player when they've been getting a bad press. Players want the publicity for themselves, they don't want their agent to be making the headlines instead of them. That's unless the player is being criticised, then they appreciate it if you get out there and are proactive in sticking up for them.

Some players care what people are saying about them and some take no notice of it at all. A lot of the players never read the papers and live in their own bubbles and if they're foreign they're more interested in the news in their own country than what's going on here. A few of them sometimes get upset about what's being said or written about them, but they're all big boys and, to a certain extent, criticism and abuse are unfortunately part and parcel of the modern game. Sometimes a player will send me or one of the other guys here a screenshot of something that's been written about him. But unless it's something serious, there's not much we can do about it. When it comes to transfer stories, some of them take no notice of it unless it's about them or their club. What they're all interested in is any stories about their club trying to sign someone in their position. You have to look after yourself.

I sometimes just can't work out why some journalists are linking a player with a club. I know for a fact the club have zero interest but I think one of the reasons journalists do it is they find out what position a club is looking to strengthen in, then they come up with a list of possible names they could sign for that position. I don't want to slag anyone off but sometimes it feels like some of them are just pulling names out of a hat.

Another reason that these links suddenly appear could be someone trying to drum up interest in a player he wants to move. If he can get the player's name out there and get him linked with clubs then it could potentially help him to set up the deal he wants.

These links appear in the media all the time and most people in the game just ignore them because we're too busy trying to do our jobs. I don't think fans take a lot of it too seriously any more either. For a start, they know that the people coming up with these stories – especially the ones on social media – aren't real journalists at all, no one knows who they really are half the time. The fans have also wised up to what is going on and they know that their club being linked with a player doesn't necessarily mean anything. Sometimes all these names being out there can cause problems for clubs, because their fans might end up criticising them for not signing players they were never in for. That's when clubs have to be proactive and use their press officers to get it out there that they have no interest in a particular player.

But doing that can cause problems as well. If a press officer briefs journalists about there being no interest in one player, then the journalists will expect briefings on all the other players the club are being linked with throughout the summer. If a club briefs that they are not interested in player A, a journalist will ask them about player B. If they say they are not going to say anything about player B, they'll think the club must be trying to sign player B. In a way, you have to feel sorry for the clubs and the press officers who are caught in the middle of it. They are damned if they do and damned if they don't.

One of my golden rules is, 'Never lie to a journalist.' You're much better off not talking to them than lying to them. Journalists have very long memories and they will never forget it if you lie to them. Depending on who they work for they have access to platforms which can reach millions of people instantaneously and, if they catch you lying to them, they can use that platform to make life difficult for you in all sorts of ways.

We're under serious pressure now from clubs to keep everything secret and not to talk to anyone about anything. They want to control everything. Sometimes they even threaten to cut your fees if news gets out about something. Journalists know the pressure we're under and they know it's nothing personal. Outside the window, when I've got a little bit more time, I'll spend more time talking to journalists on the phone. You can get lots of information out of them, they pick my brain and I pick their brain, it works both ways.

You tend to be closest to the journalists who are from the same generation as you. That's the way it used to be in the old days. Some of the older agents didn't like dealing with the younger journalists because they didn't know them, they didn't trust them and they suspected that they were more likely to write things they shouldn't write because they were trying to make a name for themselves.

In the old days, everyone in football used to read the newspapers and a paper like the *Sun* had a lot of power. Hardly anyone I know reads the actual papers now, but the media isn't just newspapers and a few TV and radio stations any more. There's all the websites and social media and hundreds of TV channels and radio stations, so you can't get away from the news even if you don't read the papers.

I read what they write online and I think most of the stuff about my players and the deals I'm working on is pretty accurate, but there are other agents who are convinced that only about 20 per cent of it is right. It's obvious that, on some deals, these social media accounts don't have a clue what they're talking about. They're guessing or they're just re-phrasing what's already out there. But on other deals, they'll get close to the truth. It all depends on who has written the story. If it's someone reliable then you can trust it, if it's one of these hit-and-miss guys or someone you've never heard of then you're not going to pay any attention to it.

The really reputable journalists know they can't afford to be wrong about anything. Before the internet and social media, if you wrote a story that was wrong, only the people who bought your paper would have read it and your story would be forgotten about the next day. Now there's no hiding place. Everything is everywhere. There is instant scrutiny on social media of everything you say or write and if you get anything wrong you'll lose your reputation very quickly. Fans on social media have very long memories and they won't forget if you get something wrong. I've seen some guys get non-stop abuse for months and months over something they got wrong.

I do actually feel sorry for journalists now because it's almost impossible for them to get close to players and managers these days. In the old days, players were normal people earning what you would call decent money – but no more than that. Some of them were on less money than the top reporters. Nowadays, footballers are in the same bracket as pop stars or Hollywood actors. A lot of them are out of reach and they've got zero interest in getting close to journalists. Most of them don't dislike journalists, they're just wary of them, they don't want to get stitched up and when they have to talk to them they make sure they give away as little as possible.

In the past, journalists would go into the canteen at the training ground to eat with the players, they'd travel to games together and sometimes even become lifelong friends. A player would talk to a journalist and he'd trust him totally. What he said would be written up in the paper without any spin and there'd be no sensationalist headlines and his words wouldn't be taken out of context. Journalists were more sure of themselves in those days, they mixed easily with the players, they may have gone to the same schools, lived on the same streets, had the same life experiences. Now, that has all changed, the footballer and the journalist live in two totally different worlds.

Why would you talk to a journalist today if you're a player unless you have to? What's in it for the player? If he's a top player, he's on TV and in the papers and on the internet the whole time anyway. He doesn't need any more exposure and he thinks speaking to journalists is more trouble than it's worth, unless he's getting paid by a sponsor to do it. One wrong word or one comment taken out of context or misunderstood and it'll be all over the papers and social media and TV.

Players speak to the media because they have to. The clubs make them do it because media access is all part of the broadcast deals. At a push, a player will put a brave face on it and go through the motions and answer a few questions about a game. He won't say anything controversial or anything that could be taken the wrong way and there's no chance he'll talk about anything to do with transfers. When it comes to the media, the most important thing as far as players are concerned is to stay off the front pages. That's the one thing they're worried about, that's the last thing they want. Write what you want about transfers, just don't write anything about their private lives.

I don't want to have a go at journalists here just for the sake of it. I'm not attacking individuals, I'm just describing the changes that I've seen in the game and in journalism since the 1970s. Journalism isn't what it used to be, but lots of things aren't what they used to be. I just wish journalists spent more time doing actual journalism, get out there and investigate properly all the things that are wrong in the world and in society instead of just churning out stories for the sake of it.

I'm reading back what I've written and I worry that maybe I'm being too harsh. Journalists have a job to do and, if they didn't do it, there are plenty of younger, cheaper versions of them who would love to take their jobs. It sounds like a perfect life, travelling around, going to games, interviewing players, being on TV and having your name in the papers every day. From what I can tell from my dealings with them, their lives are much harder than you think and the money's not great. I've got to be careful because I don't want to be too hard on them but at the same I want to be honest with the readers. I've got to get the balance right. On the one hand, journalists are an important part of the business and they do an important job covering the game for the public, but on the other hand, there are things I see which just aren't right, especially on social media.

Sometimes I just laugh at some of the stuff I see on there. I don't go looking for it because I'm from a different generation. My kids show it to me or players or people at clubs will send me pictures of some of the things they've seen on Twitter or whatever. You even get proper journalists – and by that I mean the ones from reputable papers – sending you this stuff because they want to check out that it's not true. There's one website out there that just seems to make up stories. Last week they said one of my players was going to six different clubs on six different days. I just can't get my head around why anyone would take anything they say seriously.

There's a saying which I think is so untrue. People say, 'There's no smoke without fire.' I can tell you for a fact there's plenty of smoke without fire. These stories get put on the internet and within minutes everyone is sharing them around without realising that it's probably just something that a bored kid made up in his bedroom.

I've had players calling me saying they've seen that Man United or Juventus or whatever want to sign them and we have a laugh about it. Most of the time it's harmless, but sometimes these stories can cause problems at clubs and especially in dressing rooms. People start wondering where the story's coming from and they can jump to the wrong conclusions. It can affect a player's performance and his relationship with his teammates – and it can affect a team's performances as well.

The stronger players, the ones with the right mentality, just take it all in their stride and ignore all the noise around them and their club. They know these stories are not based on any reality so they just block it all out, but it's not always that easy when you see your teammates every day and you're in a training ground with a hundred people and everyone spends hours on their phones every day seeing all this stuff.

The players all know how the game works and, when they want something, they don't have any issues with using the papers to try to get it. If a player wants a new contract or he wants a move, he won't have a problem with his agent using a PR or a friendly journalist to get some stories out to create some interest. If you can create a story that says Brighton are interested in your player, then you can go to other clubs and they'll be more interested if they think Brighton are interested as well. I'm just using Brighton as an example. It can be any club, preferably one that is doing well and has a good reputation for recruitment. You can also say to the club, 'Look, Brighton really want him, but he doesn't want to go there, he would love to come to you.'

Some agents have a reputation for operating like that because they're so desperate to do deals. Most of the time it's harmless; there's big money at stake and everyone wants a piece of the pie so everyone's going to use every trick in the book to try and get what they want. Clubs know how the game works and they all know exactly what's going on. Sometimes they'll use their media departments to brief journalists when it's in their interest. I had one situation a few years ago when someone high up at a Premier League club was unhappy about something that had been written about a player he'd bought. He called up to see if there was anything I could do to sort it. I called the journalist and he was happy to set the record straight in the paper the next day. That's the only time someone like him has ever asked me to do anything about a transfer story that was wrong.

Some of the owners, chairmen and club executives don't care what's being written about their transfer business but a few of them are very sensitive and read everything. Why, I do not know. There's so much noise and misinformation out there that the best thing to do is ignore as much of it as possible, unless it's something really personal or totally wrong. One thing they all get interested in is if they see a story that's true and they'll make calls and try and find out how it got out. A lot of the time there's so much going on though that it really doesn't matter that much to them what people are saying.

Stuff leaks out all the time and they honestly don't care. I had one player who had a release clause in his contract and only three people knew about it – him, me and the chairman. A couple of clubs wanted to sign him and suddenly a story appeared about his release clause and they had the price exactly right. The chairman was gutted because that meant he couldn't get more than the release clause for the player, but he didn't have anyone to blame but himself because he's the one who was happy to sign the deal with the release clause.

In the end, he realised there wasn't anything he could do about it. The release clause was paid and the player got his move. He was happy, I was happy, his new club were happy and the chairman got his money. Just not as much as he wanted. I still don't know how the information about that release clause got out but I know it didn't come from me or the player and it wasn't in the chairman's interest for anyone else to know, so it can't have been him.

Footballers don't need to know any journalists. Same as most chairman and owners. If you own or run a big club then you're a very rich person and you shouldn't really care that much what people are writing about you, but I suppose we're all human no matter how much money we've got. Managers do need to have good relationships with journalists because they're dealing with them and being interviewed by them almost every day. Being a good communicator is part of the job for a modern manager and, even if they can't stand the press, they have to be a big boy and put a brave face on it and go out and speak to them.

You see managers being asked questions about transfers at press conferences and you sometimes think, Why are they even being asked these questions? There's nothing they can say. They can't talk about players at other clubs because that could be seen as tapping up and they're not going to say a word about any deals their club might or might not be involved in. I can see why journalists ask the questions because that's their job. They can't enjoy it because it puts them in an uncomfortable position. They must know full well they're not going to get a proper answer but they've still got to ask the question anyway.

The transfer stories you read don't come from press conferences anyway. Stories leak out because on an average deal there will be up to twenty people involved and it only takes one of them to say something for the story to get out. If you're buying a player from a club in, say, Italy, there will be the clubs involved, the player and his agents, the intermediaries, the lawyers, the doctors and the people who draw up the paperwork. If you're working on a deal like that it's almost a given that an Italian reporter will find out and write about it.

Imagine if David Beckham wakes up one morning and thinks he wants to buy a new house. How many people know he wants to buy a new house? That's: 1.

He goes to an estate agent, sees a house he likes the look of and tells the estate agent he wants to go and see it. How many people know he wants to buy a new house now? Beckham and the agent. 1 + 1.

The agent calls the guy who owns the house and says, 'You're not going to believe this but David Beckham wants to come and have a look at your house!' How many people know Beckham wants to buy a house now? Beckham, the agent and the homeowner. $1 + 1 + 1$.

So now it's only a few hours after Beckham has woken up and thought he wants to buy a house but already $1 + 1 + 1$ people know about it. You might think that $1 + 1 + 1 = 3$ but you'd be wrong because, in actual fact, here $1 + 1 + 1 = 111$.

That's how stories get out and, the more famous you are, the more stories there are going to be out there about you. As long as what's been written about you is not personal and it's not affecting your family or your livelihood then players don't care. They live in an ivory tower, they don't give their numbers to journalists and they've got people around them who deal with the media when they have to.

Two of the days of the year when players do take a lot of notice of the media are deadline days. I'm normally too busy to watch the coverage but there have been days when I don't have much going on. A few years ago, it was so quiet that I arranged to have lunch with one of my players. Halfway through the meal, I started getting calls and messages from journalists wanting me to confirm that the player who was sitting in front of me eating salmon was having a medical at a club two hundred miles away.

Deadline day is a mad day and the media are part of the madness. I preferred it in the old days when there was no deadline. Well, there was a deadline, but it was just a few weeks before the end of the season to stop clubs buying players at the last minute to try to win something or avoid getting relegated.

It's a frustrating day now because you get calls from clubs who want to do a deal at the last minute for players you'd offered them weeks ago. I had a situation last summer where a club kept telling me they didn't want this player and then they called me on deadline day and said they wanted to do the deal. The only problem was the player was on international duty about three thousand miles away. By the time I got hold of him, there weren't any flights available to bring him back to the UK to do the deal.

I don't expect you to feel sorry for me, but the summer window also ruins any chance of having a proper holiday with your kids. It's impossible to switch off at that time of the year, it's impossible to turn off your phone and focus on spending time with the family.

I know what you're thinking. What's he got to complain about? That's a bit rich coming from an agent who's rolling in money. That's not always the case. There are thousands of agents in this country and only about a hundred are actually doing any real deals.

I went to a non-league game recently to check out a player and a guy came up to me and said he'd always wanted to meet me. We got talking and it turned out he was an agent as well. I asked him how many players he had and he said he had one. A seventeen-year-old kid who was playing in the game we were watching. I said, 'How do you making a living looking after just one player?' He gave me his card. He was the manager of the local BMW dealership.

Good luck to the guy. I've got no issue with him and I'm not looking down my nose at anyone. He's got a dream and he's trying to make it come true. Doing what I do, I get a lot of people asking me for advice. A lot of people want to work in football and they think it's going to be a dream job. I get kids who are introduced to me by friends or friends of friends and they want to know how to get into football.

I've even had a few ask me about how they can go about becoming football journalists or presenters. In the old days, you might have been able to have a word with someone you knew and try to set up some work experience for them, but those avenues seem to have all been closed off now.

I just tell them football is a great industry to work in and one of the most important things is your reputation. There are lots of good journalists out there, so read what they write and watch what they do and say and try to be like them. Be a proper journalist, don't just do it because you want to be famous on the internet or on social media.

Get real stories. Tell the truth.

Chapter 10

There's a Very Simple Explanation – I Lied

There are people out there, including some football fans, who don't like transfers. They remember a time when there wasn't such a media frenzy surrounding the buying and selling of players. The introduction of transfer windows in English football has played a big part in the explosion of interest and so has the internet and social media.

Anyone under the age of twenty reading this book will probably not know much about what life was like as a football fan in the pre-internet age. In those days, you had to rely on local and national newspapers for your fix of football news and there were no television or radio stations dedicated to the national sport. If you wanted the latest scores, you had to listen in on commercial radio stations which had sports programmes or BBC Radio 2, who crammed football into their easy listening schedule until Radio Five was launched in 1990.

Football coverage wasn't everywhere like it is today. If you wanted it, you had to go looking for it. Many fans relied on television text services like Ceefax and Teletext for news and scores and, by the 1980s, there were also phone lines you could call which cost a small fortune and charged you by the minute. The operators of these services knew that the best way to increase their profits was to keep you on the line for as long as possible. There were different numbers to call for each club and the trick seemed to be to delay revealing the big news of the day – if there was anything – for as long as possible in order to drag out the call.

The 1980s were also the golden era of fanzines, those magazines lovingly produced by fans and sold outside grounds or at bookshops like Sportspages off the Tottenham Court Road in central London. Shops like Sportspages were at the forefront of the growth of interest in new football books, like Nick Hornby's *Fever Pitch*, *Football Against The Enemy* by Simon Kuper and the classic *All Played Out* by Pete Davies about England's campaign at the World Cup in Italy in 1990.

There had been brilliant football books before – like *The Football Man* by Arthur Hopcraft, *The Soccer Syndrome* by John Moynihan and *Only A Game?* by Eamon Dunphy – but there was something fresh and exciting about the new titles which were suddenly appearing in bookshops that had rarely stocked books about football before.

Younger viewers may struggle to believe that there was a time when there wasn't live football to watch on TV every day. Before the Premier League and satellite television, games were only occasionally shown live and the ones that were tended to be big finals or major international tournaments. Children watching cup finals would secretly hope the game ended in a draw so that there would be a midweek replay on a school night which would also be shown live on TV. With little football on TV compared to what we are used to now, what was shown was unmissable if you were a fan, including highlights and magazine shows which were essential viewing for everyone who loved the game.

Not everybody did love the game in those days. Football wasn't everywhere and if you were into it sometimes it could feel like a lonely existence. You could turn up on the day and watch virtually any game you wanted and there was usually plenty of standing room for you and your mates. It's hard to believe now in the age of the £2,000 season ticket and games sold out weeks in advance, but in the 1980s you could turn up at virtually any game and pay £2 or £3 to get in.

The dearth of coverage compared to what we are now used to meant you looked forward and cherished everything about football on TV and radio and in newspapers. As for transfers, they weren't really a big deal in those days. Players were bought and sold and occasionally big sums of money changed hands but there was no window and there was very little hype. Even in the 1990s, transfers seemed to happen out of the blue. You'd wake up one morning and read in the paper that Manchester United had signed Andy Cole from Newcastle United, and a few days later you'd watch him scoring in a red shirt on *Match of the Day*.

In the old days, it didn't seem like anyone really went around looking for information about transfers and the people who were interested got what they needed from tabloid newspapers. Some people might think tabloids are downmarket, but when it comes to sports journalism and football reporting nobody can match them for the sheer number of stories they break. There was a time when they were the only people who would be out there reporting on transfer stories. Back then, broadsheet newspapers – the so-called quality press – thought that transfers were beneath them, that it was all just rumour and speculation. They would report on a deal when it had been completed and the rest of their sports pages would be devoted to match reports, features, news, analysis and comment.

Football reporting used to be a specialist skill and to end up working on a national newspaper you had to be a properly qualified journalist with years of experience on local newspapers or at news agencies. You may have got your foot in the door at a national paper by doing casual sub-editing shifts to supplement your income while working for a local paper, or you may have provided match reports for them because you worked for a news agency. Unless you were a senior journalist, nobody cared about your opinion, your job was to get stories and the only way to do that was to make contacts.

One man who made it all the way from the bottom to the top of sports journalism is Paul McCarthy. I have known him for about twenty years and when our paths crossed for the first time, he was the sports editor of the *News of the World*. The Sunday tabloids always seemed to break big football stories and the *News of the World* was the leader of the pack until it was shut down in 2011 as a result of the phone-hacking scandal.

Paul seems to know everyone in football and he has been involved in covering some of the biggest sports stories of the past forty years, so I thought it would be a good idea to talk to him about transfers. We didn't meet up just to talk about old times, I wanted to pick his brain about where his transfer stories came from and the qualities you need to find them and break them.

Paul went to sixth form college to train to become a journalist. After starting off at his local paper, the *Basingstoke Gazette*, he worked his way up via the *South London Press* to senior roles on some of the UK's biggest national papers before he become the sports editor of the *News of the World* in 2007.

One of his biggest breaks was being in the right place at the right time in 1988. While he was working at the *South London Press*, Wimbledon were gatecrashing the First Division and shaking up football with no-nonsense tactics and a dressing room full of larger-than-life characters like Vinnie Jones and John Fashanu. Covering Wimbledon as the local paper reporter was a dream job. The Crazy Gang were front and back page news – and not just in the local papers. They were beating the big boys at their own game with a fraction of their budgets and the national papers wanted stories about them. Their contacts weren't necessarily as good as the local paper reporter who covered every game and was at their training ground every day.

When Paul first started covering Wimbledon, he remembers their manager Bobby Gould taking him into the dressing room to introduce him to the players.

'This is Paul McCarthy,' Gould said. 'I want you to trust him until he lets you down, then feel free to fuck him off.'

To break stories, especially transfer stories, you need contacts and there is no better way to get them than to be invited into a dressing room and be endorsed like that by the manager in front of all his players. Nothing like that would happen these days, of course, and a club would probably call the police if you set foot in their dressing room. Times may have changed but the basic elements of the job are still the same. Stories come from you talking to people, and getting them to talk to you and trust you is the most important element of the job. There are no shortcuts when it comes to contacts. If you don't have them, you are wasting your time. One of your greatest strengths has to be the ability to get to know people in football and get them to trust you. Of course, that isn't easy and it will take you years to build up a comprehensive contacts book.

To get your own original transfer stories you will also need to spend less time focusing on everyone else's stories. There will always be big transfer stories which will dominate windows. Those are the bread-and-butter stories which everyone will be covering and you could be expected to provide updates and developments about what is going on. To make a real name for yourself though, you need your own original stories and the only way to get those is to speak to people. I don't mean speak to people every time you need something from them which could be only once a year, I mean speak to them regularly, keep in touch, keep in contact, talk about what is going on in the game, tell them what you know and what you have heard and they will tell you what they know and what they have heard. You won't get a story every time you speak to them and they probably wouldn't speak to you again if they noticed you were reporting everything they told you. You have to be discreet, you have to be selective, you have to be open and honest with them when it comes to something you want to report. And always remember that you can never write or say anything that will give your source away.

I spoke to a club owner a week before I met Paul and the phone call lasted about half an hour. Football is all we talked about and the whole conversation wasn't just about what was happening at his club. He asked me as many questions as I asked him. I asked two questions about transfers and he gave me information on two potential deals which would both be big stories. Now, I could have got off the phone to him and gone and broken those stories, but behaving like that would have jeopardised our relationship.

I didn't discuss the possibility of reporting what he had told me, so it would have come as a surprise to him if it had suddenly appeared in the media. It might also have caused a problem for him with the players and other clubs. I made a note of what he told me and, when the time is right, that information will be invaluable when I need to write or talk about those two players. Even if I never report what he told me, it's useful information for me to have, because it helps me build up a clearer picture of the transfer business his club are planning and whenever I speak or write about them, I will have background information which I can use.

The best journalists call their contacts regularly and when he was a reporter, Paul would spend four or five hours every Friday afternoon and evening on the phone to his contacts. In those days, his patch was London so he would make sure he had at least one person at every club in the capital who he could call regularly. So at least once a week – and often more – he would be in touch with contacts at West Ham United, Arsenal, Spurs, Chelsea, Wimbledon, QPR, Fulham and Watford. No call was wasted. Sometimes he would get a story, sometimes he wouldn't get a story, but he was always getting information and he was always staying in touch.

To be in a position to make those calls you have to have those numbers and those contacts, but making those connections is not easy. It will take years to build up your contacts book and you have to start at the bottom. When Paul was covering Wimbledon for the *South London Press*, he could just go to where they trained every day at the Richardson Evans Memorial Playing Fields in south-west London. Nobody is going to get that kind of access to a club these days, but there is nothing to stop you going to a club's youth and development team games to meet people and make contacts. At these games, you will be able to talk to scouts and coaches, and you might come across first-team players and coaches who are watching from the side-lines. It is also not unknown for club owners or senior executives to come and watch to see how the kids are getting on.

Up until 2012, you could also go and watch Premier League reserve teams play and that was a good opportunity to meet people. At those games there would usually be a mix of up-and-coming players and established professionals, managers and coaches as well.

'Football is a small village and people like to gossip and chat,' Paul said. 'I remember going to places like Highbury to watch Arsenal reserve games and you could go in the players' bar afterwards and introduce yourself to people. It was easy to get to know people as long as you were polite and knew what you were talking about. You introduced yourself, showed an interest in the person you were talking to and showed them you knew a bit about the game.'

You are not just there to watch a game and talk to people though. It's not a day out of the office for you to enjoy. The ultimate aim is to get numbers to increase your pool of contacts and, in the days before mobile phones, the best way to close the deal was to hand over your business card with a pen, inviting them to write down their number for you as well.

'In some ways it's more difficult to get physically close to players these days,' Paul said, 'but you do have social media and you can contact some players on things like Instagram and Twitter. There is a big gulf now between the lives of footballers and the lives of journalists. In the 1970s and 1980s, some players were earning the same kinds of wages as journalists. It was easier to get to know them because we lived in the same kinds of worlds. It is much harder to have a one-to-one relationship with a player now. You are much more likely to be close to their agent; the player will be much more remote. People forget that we used to fly in the same planes as the team to European games and the luggage carousel was always a great place to chat because everyone had to wait for their bags – no matter who you were. Journalists sat at the back of the plane and it wasn't unheard of for players to come to the back for a cigarette and a chat.'

Sports editors used to joke that the requirements for being a good football reporter were a journalism qualification and the ability to hang around car parks waiting for footballers. It wasn't actually a joke, because that was what life really was like for reporters – you could get some great stories from hanging around the players' car park after games. The trick was to know which car belonged to which player. If you knew that, you could wait by his car until he turned up and more often than not he would be happy to stop and chat for a few minutes.

It is easy to get carried away by the action and the

drama when you are at a game but your whole day is going to be one of intense concentration and hard work. You will have done plenty of preparation before the game and when it kicks off you will be concentrating on writing your match report, which may well be live and has to be filed on the final whistle. As soon as the game is over you will need to get reaction from the managers and players and write another piece or update your match report with the quotes. If it is an evening game, you will be working against the clock because newspaper deadlines are between 10 p.m. and midnight. Before laptops and WiFi and mobile phones, the only way to file your copy was to dictate it to a copy-taker on a landline telephone. Once you had done all that, you couldn't just put away your pen and notebook and go home, you would head straight for the players' bar or the car park to get quotes and material for follow-up stories.

Being a football reporter is a very tough and very competitive job. You have to be a qualified journalist and you have to know the game. You have to master the art of writing clear and concise copy in double-quick time and you have to be able to handle the pressure of meeting tight deadlines. On top of that, you need to have a nose for a story. Getting a story is the hardest part of journalism and the ability to get one is what will set you apart from everyone else.

There are Twitter accounts out there with millions and millions of followers which are purely dedicated to breaking transfer stories. Some of them are just aggregators – accounts which take information from other sources – and some of them are real journalists who are working around the clock to break stories during windows. To become trusted and respected, your stories have to be new and original and you have to have a very good strike rate. You can only get stories wrong a few times, at most, before people start to lose faith in you. Once that happens, it is very difficult to rebuild your reputation. There are people in the industry who are known to occasionally write fliers, which are stories based on very little information, written on a hunch, which may or may not turn out to be true. There seems to be more of that on social media than in newspapers these days and the vast majority of stories printed are based on real information from multiple sources.

'Only a very small percentage of transfer stories have no substance to them,' Paul said. 'A much bigger percentage have something in them. Even if a transfer doesn't happen, it doesn't mean that the story was wrong, it doesn't mean the club weren't interested in signing that player. Not every transfer happens. Clubs will have five or six targets in every position.'

A sports editor will always ask questions when a reporter comes to them with a big story. They will want to know where the story comes from, how it has been checked out, how many sources there are for it and who they are. Reporters are always reluctant to reveal their sources unless you are speaking to your editor. They are responsible for what goes in the paper and they need to trust you and you need to trust them. Without that level of trust, you are not going to last long at their paper and if you refuse to tell them who your source is then they can just refuse to print your story. You can't be precious when it comes to confiding who your source is to your editor. In time, they may stop asking you who your source is when you write about a particular club because you have told them once and they will not ask you again.

Living in the social media age means some people have become obsessed with how many followers they have on Twitter or Instagram. Even journalists who aren't officially on social media must have shadow accounts which they use just to see what is out there. Twitter is a very useful resource for journalists even if you don't want to have your own public account. There are far too many people on there who use it for self-promotion and if they irritate you, you can always just unfollow them.

If you are applying for a job, your employer is going to look at your social media accounts. In journalism, that means looking at the kinds of stories you have written and worked on in the past. It will be your ability to break stories and your reliability and reputation which will impress them more than the number of followers you have.

'If I wanted to employ someone and it was down to two reporters and one of them wasn't on social media, I'd have to think about who I was going to take,' Paul said. 'If one of them had an 85 per cent strike rate with stories and had a big following on Twitter, and the other one had a 90 per cent strike rate but wasn't on Twitter, I'd always take the one with the higher strike rate. Stories are what matters. Twitter is a great tool for reporters to use to reach out to people and to amplify their work. I'm happy for them to use it, as long as they can put up with all the filth and abuse. But if I am employing someone I want a reporter who's going to get me stories more than anything else.'

The filth and abuse directed at football reporters on social media has become a problem, so much so that it seems like some people are using Twitter less and less. That is my own personal experience. In print or on radio or TV, you explain what you have found out at some length and describe any nuances and lay out both sides of the story if there are two sides to the story. On Twitter that is not possible because you are restricted to 280 characters and the platform is designed to get people arguing with each other. The more people argue and get worked up and take sides the longer they spend on Twitter which means they see more adverts and make Twitter more money.

Footballers and journalists have had different opinions about the value and dangers of Twitter ever since it launched in 2006. Fewer and fewer footballers seem to be using it now and the ones who are on it increasingly have their accounts run by social media managers. It feels like football reporters are having doubts about it as well. The abuse can have a real effect on you and the whole platform is beginning to feel like a massive non-stop worldwide argument. It's very tempting to step back from it or walk away completely, and colleagues who no longer use it say it is one of the best decisions they have made as far as their mental health and wellbeing are concerned.

Although I am sure they look at it like everyone else who works in football, agents aren't active on Twitter at all. They will check out what people are saying but the nature of their jobs means there is nothing to be gained from being a prolific tweeter under your own name if you are managing the careers of professional footballers.

Agents and journalists use Twitter to stay across the latest news about the game, but for journalists it is also a useful tool to boost their profile and showcase their work. Agents don't need to do that and they don't need that kind of publicity. They know all about the dangers of social media and they will make sure their players receive the best possible advice about how to behave online in the digital information age. Agents and clubs will also make sure their players are taught how to behave and deal with journalists. Everybody knows players can't tell journalists everything, but they should be as open and honest as they can and as polite and friendly as possible at all times.

Although players and journalists are not as close as they were thirty or forty years ago, it still feels like a lot of players respect journalists and understand they have a job which is difficult and stressful and an important part of the game. Without the blanket coverage of the game on numerous different platforms these days, there wouldn't be the extraordinary level of interest that there is in the game, and that level of interest is what enables the top players to earn what they earn.

Part of an agent's job is to manage the public profile of his players and that is one of the reasons why they will always try to have good relations with the media. Another reason is that journalists can be very useful to have onside when it comes to transfers, although you could argue that reporters need agents more than agents need reporters during windows.

To get transfer stories, reporters need to know as many agents as possible and the nature of those relationships can appear to be very transactional. It is a case of, 'You scratch my back and I will scratch your back.' Agents use reporters and reporters use agents. Agents need reporters and reporters need agents. Some agents will be so big and powerful that they don't need to deal directly with reporters. Even at that level, there seem to be plenty of them who still like to keep close to the media and if they don't do it personally they have PR professionals who do it on their behalf.

The vast majority of agents are trustworthy when it comes to giving you information, although they will often be very reticent when it comes to talking about deals they are working on. Reporters understand that but it is still worth staying in touch regularly, because agents may have heard things and have information on deals which are not their own. Football is a very gossipy industry. People like to talk, people like to share information, people like to find out what you know. Not all of it is for reporting, but you can use it all for background information and to build up a clearer picture of what is happening at a particular club or with a particular player. We live in the information age and you need as much information as you can get in order to do your job properly.

As with any industry, there are some unscrupulous people working as agents and they will try to use journalists to help them make money. The most common way of doing that is to use at least one reporter to create a buzz and hype around one of their players. The player in question may not even be their player, they may just have a mandate from a club to buy or sell that player, so they need to drum up interest to complete a deal and make money before the window closes and their mandate expires.

Agents are a good source of information and great contacts to have along with players, managers and owners. Like other contacts in the game, it is always good to get to know agents as they are making a name for themselves. If you are starting out as a football reporter, the top agents are going to be difficult for you to have a relationship with so you may want to focus on the up-and-coming agents who are on their way to becoming big names in the business. That is not to say that you should not bother to target the more established agents, it is just that you may find it easier to build up a close relationship with agents who are on the up and who may not already have established contacts in the media.

Another question that I get asked from time to time,

although not in polite society, is whether I, or other reporters, make any money from the transfers we report on. To put it bluntly, I'm asked if I am taking a cut. I'm asked if the agents give us money for having, in a small way, helped to make a deal happen. To answer that question – which I think is usually asked as a joke or when the questioner has had too much to drink – requires only one word in block capitals with an exclamation mark: NO! I have been in this business for a long time and I have never come across or heard of a reporter who has been paid by an agent. There really is nothing more to say. Agents may be friends with reporters, they may take them out to lunch or give them some wine for Christmas, but journalists will have to declare any gifts they receive to their employers and I have never heard of a single instance of money changing hands.

There is also sometimes a misconception about what kind of journalist ends up reporting on transfers. Some people seem to look down their noses at transfer reporters. That might stem from the old days when broadsheet newspapers didn't sully their hands with anything as mucky as transfer tittle-tattle. It is true to say that the senior writers on the national newspapers don't spend too much of their time chasing transfer stories, but they have a lot of respect for their colleagues who do come up with the stories which end up on the back pages during windows. People in the industry know how difficult it is to break a big transfer story, so they respect the reporters who come up with the goods time and time again. Some of the best sports journalists in the print industry are now the ones who cover transfers. Their editors know they are invaluable because there is an insatiable appetite for transfer stories and they get eyeballs on websites and they sell papers.

There may have been a few reporters out there who got more stories wrong than right, but you don't keep your job if your strike rate is not very high when it comes to accuracy and reliability. Paul remembers one freelancer from his time at the *News of the World* whose favourite trick was selling a story to a Sunday paper which he would follow up by trying to sell a story to a Monday paper knocking down his original story. There are a few rogues in any industry and football journalism is no different. The rogues are found out pretty quickly though, especially in our new media age where information is easy to access and people are ready and waiting to jump on you on social media if you get something wrong.

Football reporters are only human and occasionally they do get things wrong unintentionally. The nature and pressure of the job means that mistakes will happen from time to time and, when they do, it won't be long before you have an angry club press officer or manager or player or agent on the phone to complain. If a genuine mistake has been made then it is, of course, standard practice for a reporter or editor to hold up their hands and apologise. Though it is not always as clearcut as that. When it comes to transfer stories, things can change very quickly. One day a deal can be hot and the next day it can have totally cooled off. That doesn't mean to say that the reporter who wrote that the deal was close the previous day was lying or making things up, or in the popular social media jargon of the day it does not mean he is a fraud.

Senior editors on newspapers will have a close relationship with their reporters and they will know where all the stories they publish are coming from. Nothing will appear in the paper unless it comes from a reliable source and has been thoroughly checked out. An editor will trust his reporters and he will have total faith in what is in his paper. If someone calls to complain, he will back his reporter unless there is clear evidence that a mistake has been made. Of course, you can check a story out multiple times with multiple sources and it can still turn out to be wrong, but not always for the reasons you may think. Sometimes even the most senior sources in the game can mislead you. Sometimes it is intentional and sometimes it is unintentional, as Paul remembered to his cost from something that happened to him thirty years ago.

'I was writing for the *News of the World* in 1993 and I was getting ready to go to Wembley to cover the FA Cup final between Arsenal and Sheffield Wednesday,' he said. 'The *Daily Mirror* and *Daily Express* had a big story that morning that Glenn Hoddle was going to be the next Chelsea manager. I knew the Chelsea chairman, Ken Bates, so I called him up to see what was going on. The stories had been written by Harry Harris and Steve Curry and they were close and I knew there was a good chance the story was right.

'Ken just said, "No, the story is not true. Whoever has written it must be drunk or on drugs. It's total rubbish and you can write that. And trust me, when I do appoint a new manager, you will be the last to know." We both laughed and, because Ken had denied the story in the strongest possible way, I rang my desk and told them what I had found out.

'On Monday, Hoddle was appointed Chelsea manager. When I had calmed down, I called Ken. He asked me how I was and I told him I was actually pretty pissed off about what had happened. He said, "Well, there's a very simple explanation – I lied."

'I was fuming and I told him he shouldn't worry if I wrote something about him in the *News of the World* in the future that was wrong because I had just lied. I remember his reply to this day: "If you lie about me, I will sue your bollocks off."'

Paul still knows Ken to this day, they made up quickly and are friends, and that just goes to show that you can't make enemies of powerful people in this business, especially if they own a club like Chelsea. You need your contacts and if they let you down you have to get over it and try to rebuild the trust between the two parties. At the same time you have to be prepared to fall out with people and upset people and rub them up the wrong way. It is all part of the job. You are trying to find things out that some people don't want you to know and they are not going to be happy if you find what you are looking for. You always have to be prepared and expect criticism from fans, readers and viewers. You just have to accept the fact that you cannot be everyone's cup of tea. Some people are going to like you and some people are going to hate you, but the vast majority of people don't care about you or what you say or do.

Of course, if you are not performing, your harshest critics are going to be the people who employ you. If you are not delivering the goods, you are going to be found out very quickly and you will be out of the door. Sports journalism is a competitive business so there will always be an army of young talent waiting to take your place.

'Football journalism is about getting out there and getting mud on your boots,' Paul said. 'That's what's going to get you stories. In the old days, the chief football correspondent at a paper would do the big interviews, the big press conferences and the big match reports. There is no demarcation any more. The number ones now have to do it all and that means breaking stories as well as everything else. As one of my former bosses used to say, "Don't give me leafy lanes, give me what's going to happen."'

By 'leafy lanes' Paul's former boss meant articles which are heavy on flowery prose and descriptions of the weather and the scenery but light on actual news. News has to be new, something that people don't already know, and it's much harder to find than a lot of people assume. Getting big exclusives in football journalism is the hardest part of the job and most of the writers who are at the top of the profession, the ones who have their own columns and go to all the big games, got to where they are because they worked hard for years and years and broke big stories. There is no short cut. It is survival of the fittest, survival of the hardest workers, survival of the most resourceful, survival of the reporter with the best contacts and survival of the one who breaks the most stories. It is not survival of the one who can best describe a leafy lane.

Chapter 11

Everybody Wants Everything

Nothing would happen in the world of transfers without owners. They are the people who ultimately decide whether to buy or sell a player and they are the ones who sign the cheques.

Getting close to them is not easy but it is part of your job as journalist to get to know as many of them as possible. If you know them well and they trust you, then you should get some useful information from them about transfers you are working on.

By and large, they will not want to give too much away and the higher up you go in the leagues, the more remote and reticent they will be. Even if they like you a lot – and I am not sure any of them like me that much – they will sometimes find it very difficult to tell you anything meaningful, even off the record.

Say a club is close to appointing a new manager and you send the owner a message asking for an update. If you are lucky, you may get a reply that just says, 'Not done yet.' That is all you will have to base your latest story on. He won't be able to tell you much more because the negotiations may well be at a delicate stage and he doesn't want the club to end up looking bad if the deal is not done.

It is an even more complicated situation with transfers, but owners do tend to be a bit more helpful if you know them well – especially about players they are not going to sign. If they are definitely not in for a player, they might let you know so that there is no chance of their supporters being misled about a particular target. If they are in for a player, they may help you out with a short, occasional update message if you keep hassling them, but most of the time they will want to keep quiet. There is too much at stake for them to risk any details coming out.

It would be impossible to find an owner of a top club who would want to speak publicly about exactly what life is like for them during a window and how they and their club handle the media. I have known many owners over the years and some of them have been very colourful characters. Some of them don't like to get involved in transfers, while some of them love getting right into the thick of the action.

I have known Richard – not his real name – for about ten years. He is one of the most hands-on owners in the business. He loves his club like a fan but he would be the first to admit that he has got as many things wrong as right over the years. Months before a window opens, he is already planning what he is going to do in the market. He has had his fingers burned a few times but his overall track record in the market is one of the best in the business:

I am firmly of the opinion that the majority of the sports journalists in this country are very knowledgeable and, when it comes to football, they do a very good job of covering the game and all the stories around it.

I would like to make a distinction here between what I would call the old school type of newspaper journalists and the people you see now operating solely on social media. Unfortunately, fewer and fewer people are buying newspapers these days. I don't think I've ever seen any of my children read or take any interest in the papers which we have around the house.

They are from a different generation and they have been programmed to believe that news is consumed on phones and tablets. I am still old-fashioned. I still like to have a cup of tea in the morning with a couple of the papers in front of me. I watch TV, listen to the radio and look at the websites that everyone else looks at for football news, but my day always starts with me reading two or three real newspapers.

I am naturally drawn to anything that is written about my own club and I have to say that, when it comes to news stories during a season, what is written in the papers is usually pretty accurate. It is only when the transfer silly season starts that the stories become, how shall I put it kindly, a little bit more hit-and-miss. Some of the stories I read, especially on the internet and social media, are basically just totally made up. There is no truth to them whatsoever. I sometimes read that we are interested in a particular player, and quite often it is someone I have never heard of before. I occasionally call the manager just to check if he has any interest in the player and he just laughs and says I must have been spending too much time on my phone again.

I do get surprised sometimes when a story appears about us and it is totally right – especially if the negotiations over the deal are at an early stage. Only three people here really know when we make a serious effort to sign a player – me, the manager and the chief executive. I am not naive and I know how it all works. There may well be a lot of media noise around a particular player before we make our move, and there are so many people involved in deals now that you almost have to expect that there is a strong chance that news about what you are doing will leak into the media. There are some agents who try to use the media and clubs to drum up interest in their players. I think journalists and supporters are much more careful about what they believe these days. That is a good thing because, when it comes to transfers, you have to be very careful who you believe.

What you read in the newspapers and see on TV or hear on the radio is pretty reliable. The reputable newspapers are less sensationalist on transfers and they are often more careful and cautious with what they write until something is actually agreed. They seem to ignore a lot of the rumours that you see flying around the place.

My wife tells me that I should stop reading the papers and looking at football websites. She doesn't see the point in paying attention to people who are criticising you. Sometimes it worries her more than it worries me and she doesn't even read it, she just hears about what people are writing and saying. What can hurt and affect you is some of the comment pieces you read which are really personal. I'm not sure some journalists realise how much harm they can do with what they write.

We are all doing our best and as far as I am concerned owning and running this club takes up a lot of my time and money. When all you are getting is abuse then that can have a really big effect on your life and the lives of the people close to you. No matter how strong you are or how resilient and thick-skinned you are, being attacked by journalists who whip up fans is not a pleasant experience.

These comment pieces and all this vitriol appear when the team are not doing well or when people think you are not spending as much as your rivals. I don't mind criticism as long as it is constructive and balanced and not personal or vindictive. I don't know any owner or chairman who wakes up in the morning and decides to buy a bad player or sell a good player or appoint a bad manager. We are all doing our best and we all make mistakes. I don't mind being held to account, but if you are going to abuse me personally then I'm not interested in anything you have to say.

In most businesses, if someone said the things about you that you get called in this business then you would never speak to or deal with them again. In my experience, it can be counter-productive if you do that in football. As much as it might hurt, you have to turn the other cheek. Years ago, I was tempted to ban a few journalists because they were taking things far too far. Luckily, I was advised that it would be a bad idea because it would give them more attention and they would use being banned as a badge of honour. I've never banned anyone but I'm not sure that's something I should be proud of, considering some of the stuff that's been written about me. Whatever people write or say, we still have to let them into games for nothing, give them food and drink and let them speak to the manager and the players. When you put it all like that, being a football reporter sounds like a nice job, even though I've heard the money is not great.

When it comes to transfers and the deals we are really serious about, we are playing a game within a game with the media. We are trying to keep things under wraps and they are trying to find out what we are up to. It's in our interest to keep things quiet, because we don't want other clubs to come in for a player we are trying to sign. We gain nothing from it being in the public domain but that doesn't mean there aren't other people in the deal who don't have an interest in the news being leaked. They might want to encourage an auction so they make more from the deal, or they do it to get a better contract for the player, from you or from someone else.

Fans have become more and more obsessed with transfers because it's human nature to always want to be chasing a dream. They think if we just sign another five players in the summer then we'll win something. Everyone has an opinion on who you should buy and how much you should be spending. I think people lose sight of the fact that, in all likelihood, the players you sign are going to be worth less when the time comes to sell them – if there is anyone out there who wants to buy them and if they haven't just run down their contracts so they can leave for nothing.

If you've got a really good player, you know that bigger clubs are going to come in for him and, depending on the length of his contract, the balance of power will shift pretty quickly from you to the player and his agent. You're in a no-win situation if he's got two years or less left on his deal, because his value is going to start depreciating quickly and everyone knows it. People say, 'You should have got him to sign a new deal,' but that's not as easy as it sounds. You can offer some of these players incredible contracts worth a fortune, but they won't budge if they've decided with their agent that they're going to get a bigger contract somewhere else and a massive signing-on fee by running down their deal.

It's not all about money though. I've had players come to me almost begging for a move because of a personal problem. Sometimes they just want to go somewhere else because they want a new challenge or they want a change of scene. We're all human at the end of the day. You would need to have a heart of stone not to let some of these players leave when they ask to go. When it comes to personal problems, they're too sensitive and private to be discussed in public so if he's a player the fans like then you're going to be the one who gets the blame for letting him go.

Agents keep telling me they never leak anything and most of the leaks come from clubs but I'd be very surprised if that was the case here, especially with players we're trying to sign. There are always going to be leaks from training grounds because so many people work there, but very few of them will know about what business we are really trying to do.

Transfer windows and the whole transfer market takes up more and more of my time even when I've got a big recruitment department here. The demands of agents are never-ending. Some days it's just impossible for me to deal with the volume of calls, emails and messages I'm getting. It's impossible to delegate and leave it to others to deal with, even if you have a very good chief executive, because at the end of the day a lot of agents still want to deal with me as much as possible.

On top of that, you've got journalists who are getting your number or email address from who-knows-where trying to get information out of you as well. Journalism has changed so much, so quickly that you can't really afford to let people get close to you. There are still some journalists I've known going back years and years, the ones who call you not just to get a story out of you but to have a real conversation. You know they wouldn't mind getting a story out of you as well but they go about things the right way. There are a few of them I see once or twice a year for lunch or dinner. I might end up looking stupid if I say they're friends, maybe all they want from me is information. I don't know, all I do know is that I see them sometimes and most of the time they pay. It's always good to keep in touch with people and hear what they've been hearing. You would not believe the stories some of these journalists tell you – all strictly off the record though – the stories that have been hushed up or they're just not allowed to print.

One thing I'm always happy to talk to journalists about is the cost of the deal after it's been done. I think it's important for the real figure to be out there, so I'll always help out when I'm asked after it's all been done. The selling club always put out a bigger figure to make it look like they're getting something that was too good to turn down and the buying club puts out the lowest price possible to make it look like they're getting a good deal. That happens all the time, which is why I think it's important to get the right number out there so our supporters get the truth. Getting the right price is not always easy because there are so many add-ons and bonuses in deals these days that you sometimes don't know the exact cost for years.

I try to make sure the right prices we've paid are out there, but I'm not sure that's a good thing. In an ideal world you wouldn't want anyone to know how much we've paid for some of the players we've signed. When you start out owning a club you can lose your way and a lot of money buying players. As soon as agents find out you've bought a club they will all be in touch constantly to try and get you to sign their players. Before you know it, you've bought a load of players who turn out to be rubbish and you've got the same fans who were singing your name a few months back turning on you and the board.

I never understand why fans are so obsessed with the board in football. There is no board, there's just whoever owns the club, it's his money and he makes the decisions. I don't think people will ever understand what it feels like to waste your money on transfers. Every transfer is a risk, every single one. There's no such thing as a risk-free transfer. They all look good to begin with – that's why you sign them – but the more time you spend doing this, the more you learn not to get carried away no matter who you sign.

You have to sign players every summer to progress as a club. Everyone is encouraging you to spend money, which is easy to do when it's not their money. You get a new manager and he wants to bring in his own players using agents he's close to. What happens to those players if you sack the manager or he leaves? I don't think anyone, except other owners, will understand what it feels like to spend millions on players who turn out to be useless. No matter how useless they are, they've signed contracts you have to honour. You have to pay them every month and getting rid of them, even for a big loss, is sometimes impossible. If you don't know what you're doing, you'll make mistakes which will haunt you for years and if you do know what you're doing, you will still make mistakes which will haunt you for years.

The two deadline days are two of the worst days of the year for me. There is so much stress and pressure. You're trying to stay calm while everyone around you is losing their heads. Your day starts at about 6 a.m. and it finishes in the early hours of the next day. You are shattered the following day, you just want to turn your phone off and lie down in a dark room. You want to get away from it all but there's just no escape from football. If you've had enough, all you can do is sell the club and get out, but that can take years and years and unless you get lucky it will be even more stressful than buying or selling a player.

I've had all sorts of abuse from fans. Most of it is on social media and, to a certain extent, you can try to block it out. That's not easy at a game when thousands of people are singing about you. All you can do is just sit there and take it all on the chin. And you have to keep taking it on the chin when videos of it are all over the internet. I have no problem speaking to fans, as long as it is done privately or in a proper forum where people aren't filming. Me arriving at a game or leaving is not a proper forum. I'm interested in having an informed and civilised conversation and debate. I am not interested in trending on Twitter because I've been ambushed by people who want to make me look stupid.

Communication with fans is always something that is difficult to get right. When things are going well, they tend to leave you alone and the spotlight is somewhere else. It's when things are not going well that all the problems start. When I started, I used to make a point of always trying to have a good relationship with the local paper. I thought that was the best way of communicating with the fans. The local paper reporters are the ones who come to every game and every press conference, they are writing about your club every day and that's where the real fans used to get their information from.

That's all changed now because the internet has killed off so many local papers. Fans get their information from lots of different sources now and local papers are struggling to survive. It's impossible to have any kind of relationship with most of the people who are writing about you and your club now. Once in a while, you'll be asked to do an interview and I have to politely decline because they're more trouble than they're worth. Everything you say can be used against you so it's just best to say nothing at all. There has to be an element of trust before you agree to be interviewed and that no longer really exists because football has become so big and the interest in the game is almost unmanageable.

Don't get me wrong, I still think there are some good, reliable and reputable journalists out there. They are knowledgeable and I read what they write, even their transfer stories. If I could, I would talk with them more openly more often, but that's not possible because we live in a media-saturated age and being in the spotlight is emotionally and mentally draining. The world keeps changing and not everything changes for the better.

The people I feel sorry for during transfer windows are our media department. They are the ones at the frontline dealing with the press. They're getting hundreds of calls from journalists all over the world asking them for information about all sorts of different players we're supposed to be signing or selling. I think a lot of the time they are fishing for information and it's a thankless task for our media people to deal with it all. They try and help and steer when they can but, realistically, there's not much they can say.

If it's a credible name that we are being linked with, they'll contact our recruitment department or chief executive or me to find out what we should be saying. Sometimes we tell them to kill a story and sometimes we tell them to let it run. You're always thinking about the interests of the club first and then the fans. Our media team tell me about 80 per cent of the names they're asked about are total fliers, there's absolutely no truth in the story they want to run and it's obviously information which they have got from an agent. The reputable journalists won't run the story if we tell them that there is no truth in it, but some of the others, especially the younger ones who are trying to make a name for themselves, go with it anyway or they don't bother to call you to check in the first place. I think these younger journalists think it's much easier to ask for forgiveness than it is to ask for permission. They call up the press office after they have written something that's totally wrong and they try to apologise by saying they were under pressure.

As I said before, the vast majority of journalists do a very good job and what they write is very accurate but, like in any walk of life, there are a few people who can give the whole industry a bad name. What the ones who speculate and write things which are not based on facts don't realise is that what they are doing can sometimes have serious consequences, especially if they're talking about clauses in contracts which don't exist. Information like that being out there can harm negotiations, and when you see something that's totally wrong it just reinforces it in everyone's minds that talking to the media about transfers is more trouble than it's worth.

Everything that's written about our club is read and collected and I'm sure that's the same at most other clubs. If I've got the time, I'll look at the daily round-up and if something has got out which should have stayed in the building then we'll look at it internally. Most of the time there's no point even having an investigation because you know where it's come from. Nine times out of ten it will be a player speaking to his agent and the agent then speaking to the press. I'm sure the agents see it as a quid pro quo – they are doing the journalist a favour and they will expect a favour in return.

There's a feeding frenzy with big deals and, as the negotiations drag on, people become more and more desperate for new information and they all want to be the first journalist to break the story when the deal is done. I can understand why fans get frustrated waiting for a deal to be confirmed because these things can drag on for a long time. Deals are very complicated now and the negotiations can be very protracted. We always have to make sure that we are doing the best deal we can for the club, so it's going to take as long as it's going to take to make sure we get everything right.

I can understand why journalists want to break the story first when a signing is confirmed. It's good for their reputation and it will impress their bosses. But the people in our media department need to impress me and all our commercial partners too. They are paying us for exposure, they are paying to have their names on our shirts and, from a communications and commercial perspective, it's vital that we are first with the story, the images, the video and the interview. We don't want someone on social media or a TV or radio station or a newspaper website taking away our glory.

I've said it before and I will say it again, the club has to come first and then the fans and our sponsors and partners are part of the club and we always have to think about their interests as well. For the sake of our fans and our partners, it's important that news about signings comes out on our own channels first. I'm sorry but that's just the way it has to be. We need to get eyeballs on the brands who are paying us and one of the best times to do that is around the new signings. We have social media people who put together announcement campaigns and there's no point them doing all that work if we're just going to give everything to the newspapers and TV. The traffic to our website and social media spikes around major signings, and the more people we have engaging with our content the more money we can make for the club from selling sponsorship.

It's absolutely vital for us as a business that we can trust the people who work for us and that means confidential information has to stay inside the building. I don't want to make it sound like *Big Brother*, but everyone is being watched and that includes managers. They are given a briefing sheet by our media team with a list of the players we have been linked with and they are given clear instructions to give nothing away in interviews and press conferences. They have to stick to the line that we never comment on speculation. Sometimes a member of the media team will come and see me or call me to see if there are any specific messages we want to get out about players in a press conference.

While managers don't lie in press conference, they do have to choose their words very carefully. Having a foreign manager who doesn't speak very good English can be a double-edged sword. Sometimes it benefits the club, because their English is not good so they don't say much and that keeps us out of the headlines. But sometimes their lack of good English can lead them to say the wrong thing and that can get us a lot of bad press.

I said managers don't lie but I have to admit that there are times when they have to be cute. If we have a player who someone else is trying to sign, then he knows he has to sing the player's praises and tell everyone how good he is and how important he is for us. That usually means we end up getting a few million more when we sell the player. We had a manager say that there was no way this player would be sold, no way at all. We sold him a couple of weeks later and we got £3 million more than we would have sold him for.

The line that managers absolutely cannot cross in public is to talk about our budgets. We always back our managers when it comes to signing players, but it can't just be the players they want. The final decision about who we sign is taken by three people: the manager, me and the chief executive. Complaining about not being backed is completely counter-productive and so is briefing against the club to journalists. We've had managers in the past who've done that and they haven't lasted long.

Our current manager is very good at dealing with the press and he knows what he can and can't say about buying and selling players and budgets. So far, we trust him. Who knows what will happen in the future, because we've been in the same situation before, where the manager is happy and then he's not happy. As soon as they hit a bad patch, they start looking for excuses and other people to blame except themselves.

On a few occasions, I've had to go and speak to the communications director or a press officer to find out what went wrong in a press conference or in an interview. I've even gone straight to a manager and told him, 'Thanks for that. Thanks for telling the world that we're not giving you enough money. Putting pressure on me to protect your reputation is not going to get you anywhere.'

To a certain extent, I do have a degree of sympathy for managers. They are under extreme pressure a lot of the time and on top of all their commitments they have to be constantly speaking to the media the whole time. Some days, there are as many journalists and cameramen at the training ground as players. Everyone wants a piece of the manager and everyone wants a piece of our players. Everyone wants everything. I remember in the old days you'd have one guy from the Press Association and a couple of local newspaper reporters and that would be that.

I actually have a lot of respect for real journalists and you always have to be aware of what the opinion-formers are writing. I have no problem with what they write about the game, no problem at all. The issue I and a lot of other people have is when they make it personal and start attacking you based on assumptions which are not based on facts. I call it friendly fire. Some of these guys are at every game and every press conference, and they try to get to know everyone and everything, but at the first hint of trouble – like a few bad results – they sit at their laptops and play to the crowd by writing about things they know nothing about. They go whichever way the wind blows. I have a lot more respect for journalists who stick to what's happening in the game and some of them can write about that very well.

The ones who cause you a lot of problems are the younger generation who seem to write most on websites and social media. Even a story that people might think is not a big deal can cause problems for us and the manager. I've had a situation where an agent has called me up to see what's going on because he's read somewhere that we may be willing to listen to offers for our goalkeeper, and at the same time the player has gone to see our communications director to ask him the same question. I told the agent there was nothing in it and the player was given the same information after our communications director had contacted me about it. All this happens because someone has written something without getting their facts right. You tell the player the story's not true, you tell his agent the story's not true, but half the time they don't believe you.

At the most basic level, transfers are all about keeping the prices as low as possible for the players you are trying to sign and as high as possible for the players you are trying to sell. A lot of clubs use the media to try and get what they want. Sometimes you do that by getting stories out there and sometimes you do it by downplaying what's already out there. If you are trying to sign a player, letting everyone know about it can put the price up and get other clubs interested. If you are trying to sell a player, letting everyone know can drum up interest but it can also lead to his price falling and other clubs beginning to question why you want to let him go: 'If he's so good, why are they so desperate to get rid of him?'

Whether we like it or not, the media are a big part of transfers now. I'm sure they like it more than we do because it gets them a lot of readers and clicks and that's how they make their money. When you think about it, transfer news is one of the few areas of football that clubs haven't been able to make money from. The media dominate it and there's been a big explosion of interest since I've been here.

Some of the journalists can be a pain in the arse. They are like a dog with a bone and, in a way, you have to admire their tenacity when they are after a story. The older ones tend to be more professional, I used to like it when they wore suits and ties. Some of the younger ones these days look like they've dressed to go clubbing.

There are also a few of them who are masters of self-promotion. That's a new phenomenon, that didn't happen before. Those guys had big egos and they loved having their pictures in their papers above their articles and they saw themselves as real voices of authority in the game. Sometimes I wonder how we have gone from that to some of these people putting pictures of themselves up on social media all the time and trying to make a name for themselves by writing and talking about things they really don't know about. I'm not sure if they are journalists or influencers. Sometimes it is hard to tell the difference.

I've been asked to write down my thoughts on transfers and how they're reported, and to talk about deadline days and what they've become. The moment I look forward to most is 1 a.m. on the night of deadline day when I'm driving home thinking to myself, Thank God that's over for another six months. Ideally, you want to be in a position where you're not doing anything on deadline day except tying up a few things like players going out on loan. It all depends on how your season has gone and how your window has gone and whether you're in for any players.

Everyone wants to be like Manchester City. No mad scrambles on deadline day. If we have a quiet deadline day, I know we've had a pretty good window and there's been no panic. A quiet deadline day with nothing much happening means you did all your groundwork properly before the window opened and everything has gone according to plan.

Having to do business on deadline day is often not a choice but a necessity. A deal you have been working on could collapse at the last minute and you have to make a late move for an alternative target. You might get a late bid for one of your players which is too good to turn down and you have to move late to sign a replacement. Or you pick up an injury and you need to sign a player as a replacement and to keep the manager happy.

You can end up spinning a lot of plates on the day or you might end up having a nice day sitting back and watching your rivals flailing around trying to sign players left, right and centre. Sometimes you really don't have much of a say in how the day is going to pan out but you have to be prepared for every eventuality.

I'm actually amazed by how much of a national obsession deadline days have become. It's become like Valentine's Day. Nobody really wants to be part of it but the pressure to get involved sometimes just gets too much.

Chapter 12

I Am the Money

When I was studying to become a journalist many moons ago, it was always drummed into me that I had to be fair, accurate and impartial. That is something I have always remembered and I hope I have stuck to those principles of fairness, accuracy and impartiality throughout my career working in newspapers and on TV and radio.

When I have made a mistake, I have tried to hold my hands up and learn from it. The nature of the job I do, broadcasting live for hours every day, usually without a script, means there is always a real and present danger of things going wrong. They occasionally do because nobody is perfect and no football journalist knows everything there is to know about every story.

It is only in the last twenty or so years of my career that reporting on transfers has become a big part of my job. I sometimes think about whether it's really possible to be totally fair, accurate and impartial about transfers. After all, there are so many people with vested interests involved and so many agendas and so much secrecy that it is often increasingly difficult to get a real handle on what's going on.

Being impartial when reporting on transfers is not difficult. I know fans care passionately about their clubs and I will always make sure I treat all clubs and fans with the respect they deserve. For example, I remember being asked in the summer of 2022 who had had a better window – Spurs or Arsenal? I think I politely explained that I didn't want to get involved in any local rivalries and only time would tell who had done the best business.

You always want to be fair and accurate when you are a journalist and when I am working on a transfer story there is always a voice in the back of my mind reminding me to be fair to the player, his agent, the clubs and the fans. It would make my job easier if all of them would speak to me, but you just have to accept the fact that most people involved are not going to want to speak to the media until the end of the process.

Twenty years ago, I would never have guessed that there would be so much interest in transfers in the future. My main passions growing up were football and journalism, and a few other things; they certainly weren't transfers. But as a journalist you have to adapt and move with the times and I know a lot of people now associate me – if they know me at all – with transfers and deadline day.

I love reporting on transfers, I love the thrill and the buzz especially when I, or one my colleagues, has real, breaking news. At the same time I can understand and appreciate why some people don't like transfers at all. After all, how can it be right in this day and age when so many people are struggling to pay their bills for clubs to spend these obscene amounts of money on transfer fees and wages?

You would be surprised at how many people in the media have mixed emotions and I sit next to one of them five days a week. Simon Jordan is the co-host of my radio show and he knows what he is talking about because he used to own Crystal Palace. He is known for having forthright opinions on virtually everything and you won't be surprised to discover that he has a lot to say about how deals are done and how they are reported.

I wanted to make sure that I was fair and accurate and impartial in this book, and when researching it I tried to speak to a wide range of people with a wide range of views. Many people I spoke to – apart from agents – seemed to dread windows and transfers even though they worked in the football industry. Simon doesn't like transfers and he doesn't like the transfer business, so in the interests of balance I asked him to sit down with Kaveh and I to talk transfers.

Q. What do you think about the quality of football journalism at the moment?

A. I think it's got better recently. I think in recent times, in historic times, I don't think it's been great. I don't think it's been particularly informed or educated. And certainly when I'm doing the broadcasting I'm now doing, it's a great space for me to operate in, because it gives me a unique selling point, because I have the level of knowledge that a lot of football journalists don't have. They trot out platitudes and statistics as examples of how football works without the necessary knowledge behind it. But then again, why would you expect a journalist to have real world experience?

What I don't like about journalism, and what I don't like about football journalism, is that opinions are wrapped up as facts. They're not facts, they're just opinions. I had this great desire to have patronage for the local press over the national press, because I believed that the local press were the lifeblood of a football club and they were entitled to the relationship with a football club that was useful. And they were the most disingenuous, divisive bastards I ever met and actually it was the national press that were slightly better. That's like football full stop. It's the ones that you think you can rely on, the ones that should be on your side, they are normally the ones that let you down the most. The opposition is the ones we should be fighting against. So I always felt that there was a divisiveness about it, not necessarily a motivation to support a nuanced argument. It's very binary. It's black or it's white. It never has any context but, having said that, there are now some journalists writing articles that are interesting, engaging and more expansive than they once were before.

The relationship that the media has with football now is a marriage made in hell, but it's also a marriage of convenience because one needs the other. There is a lot of media interest in football now and subsequently there is a lot of hyperbole and mysticism and bullshit.

Q. **When you owned Crystal Palace, how much of what was written about the club was accurate, do you feel?**

A. I took very little notice of it. I took exception to some of it, but took little notice of it. I found it irritating at times. What you want is a fair crack of the whip, a fair opportunity. You don't want agendas being served out. Some journalists had agendas and some just wanted to break stories. Some wrote stories which were completely untrue and some wrote stories to try to destabilise the club before big games.

But it's a difficult one now, because my view has slightly changed. People like me don't reform, they just maybe run out of wind and get a little bit more placid about things. My attitude towards the media then was complete and utter intolerance. I wanted them to be accurate and I wanted them to act with integrity.

Q. **How do you think transfer stories were covered when you owned Palace? Were the stories accurate? Did the media know what you were up to?**

A. I don't think being accurate was their intention. The intention was to create noise. That's what the transfer window is. I hate the transfer window. I understand why people find it intriguing but, from a commercial standpoint, sitting in the transfer window, trying to do business, trying to keep control of the direction of travel, trying to keep control of a very difficult process, the more people are aware of it, the more it becomes challenging.

Ultimately the fans get involved, and all of a sudden there's an expectation you're going to sign this player, irrespective of what the player does or doesn't want.

So it's one of those businesses where you're doing your business in public and you wouldn't buy a house in public, would you?

Q. **When you saw stories linking you with players and some of the business that you were doing was ending up in the paper, did it used to annoy you? Did you try to get to the bottom of where it had come from?**

A. Yes, but it was a fruitless exercise because it was like trying to nail jelly to a wall. It used to create a feeling of malcontent and unease and disruption because you're thinking to yourself, these conversations that have been reported, some of them are close to the truth. So it creates a culture of not knowing who to trust. Who can I trust? Who's working with me? Who's working against me?

I wouldn't run my life based on what a newspaper article says, but you begin to question whether you can trust people and you wonder how the information is finding its way into the public domain. Nobody knew about some of the things I wanted to do but it ends up in the papers.

Also, instead of writing about football, some of them were writing about my personal life and the colour of my hair and I didn't see what that had to do with Crystal Palace.

Q. **What do you think of transfer reporting at the moment? What do you think about how big it has all become?**

A. I think there are some people who have accurate information. There are some people who are worth listening to and some people who aren't. Whether I like it or I don't, sport is now entertainment. It's on a different level to where it once was before.

I believe that sport should be for sport but now it is entertainment and one of the unintended consequences of the transfer window is that it has been extremely beneficial for the media and slightly beneficial for football.

All it has done is profited agents and profited players and created uncertainty in the football ecosystem. The windows are almost like a restriction of trade. In every other business, you can sell things when you want to but in football where you need to be able to bend and flex, you can only sell at pre-designated times and then get subjected to the forces of the market place.

Q. **Would you prefer to get rid of the window altogether?**

A. Totally. Have it open all year and close it in March for the last two months of the season. That's the way it used to be and there was nothing wrong with it. When football clubs ran into problems in, say, October or November, they could sell a centre-forward to pay some of their bills but that opportunity has now gone. I get the reasons why they brought it in but it has been bad for football and great for the media.

Q. **Looking back at your time at Palace, what was the best deal you did?**

A. In my world at that time, it would be selling Clinton Morrison to Birmingham City and Andrew Johnson coming the other way. It came about because Steve

Bruce wanted Clinton at Birmingham because he thought Clinton was a top player when he worked with him at Palace. Birmingham wanted Clinton when they got promoted and I already knew that Steve rated him highly so I made sure that we got top dollar. They actually offered me £5 million before they got promoted and for some reason they reduced the offer to £3.5 million after they got promoted.

Clinton wanted the move but we had reached an impasse. It was broken when we agreed to take a player as part of the deal and I wanted Andrew Johnson and we got him in exchange. Andrew ended up playing for England and he scored thirty-two goals for us one season, he ended up being the highest scoring English player in the Premier League one season and he ended up being sold to Everton for the best part of £9 million. So that was a deal that worked and it worked, with all due respect, because I did it.

Q. **What do you think about the way players behave during the window? Does it bring out the worst in them?**

A. It depends on the player. I think it's unfair to generalise and assume all players behave in the same way. There is a common trait though, which is they want what they want when they want it. But some of them accept they can't have what they want when they want it.

Andrew Johnson is case in point. He wanted to go when we were relegated and I told him you are not going but in exchange for that I will give you a pay rise, you will stay on a longer-term contract and if we don't get promoted straight away, then you can go and you can choose the club you want to go to which is what he did.

You have to be fair but in football, generally speaking, you will always have people who will disappoint you, people who will do nothing but then expect a pay review every quarter.

Q. **What do you think about transfer fees now?**

A. I think it's obscene. One of the problems with transfer fees is that they are a natural signpost for wages, because you don't pay £100 million for a footballer and then put him on £50,000 a week. You pay £100 million for the player and you pay the same amount in wages. Even though the transfer fees are inflated, they're capitalisable. You can stick them on your balance sheet. They have some inherent value, right? And there will be a market for when you may sell the player in the future and so you can retain some integral value on your investment. Wages, though, are just a straightfor-ward, bottom-line drain on profits, and they're what will underpin the challenges that you may have economically in the future.

I've never had a problem to some extent, within reason, with players getting top money. I want them to be worth what they're paid and paid what they're worth. The problem is, you paid them and they weren't often worth what they were being paid. It was a one-way transaction. When I was trying to negotiate deals with agents it was like trying to negotiate with a union leader or a terrorist. You try to find a solution, you try to give something and get something back but what agents do is take everything you give and give you nothing back. You try and find a deal to move things along. You show some goodwill and there's no goodwill coming back. So the goodwill is just yours, and that's not goodwill, that's just foolishness.

Q. Did you think you were a good negotiator or was it just take it or leave it?

A. It depended on my mood, but I was a dealmaker and that's a terrible thing to be because I wanted to do deals. I will try to make deals happen and I don't like deal-breakers and that's what agents often are, because they're not looking for solutions. They're looking for a one-dimensional outcome and then they're looking to charge you for the privilege, but you didn't work for me. You work for the other fellow. You provide his solution. Charge him. You didn't provide anything for me. 'Oh, I did. I got the player to sign for you.' Yes. At three times the price I wanted to pay. How is that working for me?

I was a victim of my own desire. If I had somebody in a room, it was because I wanted to do a deal. So what I learned very quickly was to get out of that room and stick somebody else in there, not because they could negotiate better than me, because they couldn't, but because I wanted to do a deal, I would be predisposed and have the proclivity to want to do that deal. So I'd stick the chief executive in the room to keep the money out of the room. The chief executive goes in there with a ceiling and he tells them he can't go higher because the owner out there won't give him any more money. So he gets the opportunity to be able to pause, whereas I am the money. I kept out of the room because there's no win with agents. There's no solution being provided. There are a few good ones out there, of course there are, but the fact I can list them on one hand tells you how many of the other ones are problematic.

Q. We've talked about journalists and players and agents. What are managers like to deal with during windows? How do you handle them and how much is it what they want and how much is it what you want?

A. It should never be what the owner wants besides the economics of it. The big thing with managers is that the very people that are supposed to be on your side are often not. You can get managers who go out and complain to the press about not getting what they wanted. That creates a culture of disharmony because they are concerned that they are going to be judged by the team's performance, which, by the way, they should be. And they will be judged if they didn't do their job particularly well in terms of recruitment and scouting and ended up just taking sniper shots at top-end players we weren't going to get. It wasn't because I wasn't prepared to do the deals – they didn't want to come.

There's two transfer windows. There's the ebullience and optimism of the summer transfer window, where you're building and you don't know what's coming but you're full of optimism. And then there's the January transfer window where, especially if you're struggling, you're in a situation where it's bleak and you're trying to buy your way out of a particular problem. You're trying to find a Band Aid and your manager's throwing anything into the mix. You keep hearing the phrase 'Let's get some bodies in the building.' It doesn't matter if they're any good and how much they cost.

Q. **What do you think of the way transfers are covered now? Do you miss being involved in them?**

A. Now that I'm involved in the media, I have a much greater appreciation of it than I had before. They were a necessary evil to me that served no greater good but when you become older and wiser and you see it for what it is, you see that everyone's doing a job and it's a job to be done. I have more tolerance of it now. I had scant tolerance of it before. I just thought it was a distraction. I thought it was an exercise in people showboating inside football, people wasting one another's time all for the delectation of the media.

I think the quality of journalism and the quality of reporting has gone up and there's some really good journalists out there who really understand things. As far as I'm concerned, I bring first-hand experience because I have owned and run a football club so I don't need to prove anything to anyone.

I said this a few years ago. Which journalists have ever bought a football club? Which journalists have ever played for a football club? Which journalists have ever bought a player? Which journalists have sold a player? Which journalists have been in the dressing room? Which journalists have ever hired or fired a manager? None of them. I tell you what you journalists know, what someone else tells you. That's what you know.

That was sort of my default position for a long time, but my attitude has changed because I think there's more maturity about the football industry now. If you look at the way football clubs have evolved, if you look at the way football clubs operate now in terms of business, in terms of player recruitment, in terms of the intelligence behind who they appoint and who they don't appoint.

It's not so much of a back-of-the-fag-packets, you know, find out by experience rather than doing your due diligence. So naturally, what it's done is like in a high tide boats rise – it's made journalists have to be better at their jobs. I think journalists generally should be braver. I get frustrated that journalists just stay in their lane sometimes and don't really push the envelope.

Q. **What do you make of the explosion of interest in transfers on social media?**

A. I don't think it's a good or bad thing. It's a fact of life. I think the mainstream media is in a very invidious position now because social media paints the picture and mainstream media colours it in, it follows it.

Social media gives people instantaneous information. There is no barrier to output. People can tell you whatever they want. I don't think much of it. I think it's a cesspit like most people think it is.

The two biggest commodities in football are money and gossip, aren't they? And they run neck and neck. So make of that what you will. Now, whatever forum delivers that is going to do well. When it's transfer stories on social media, the quality of the information depends entirely on the sources. I don't know these guys. I know them by association now and I don't pay much attention to them but they seem to get it right more often than not.

Q. **Finally, what do you make of transfer deadline day?**

A. I hated it. As an owner, you don't enjoy it. I have to be honest, I would try and stay out of the country on transfer deadline day. I'd be away. I didn't want to be part of it because, if I'm doing business on deadline day, I'm really moving into the territory of the last chance saloon. If you're buying players on deadline day then you are investing money – I use the term investing very loosely – on things at the last minute.

I wouldn't turn my phone off. If I don't want to speak to someone, I don't have to answer the phone. I would prefer to not be in a position where my business was being run through the media.

It's a noisy space and there's so much noise to be made because of the nature of the beast, because of the industry, because it is full of sensationalism and hyperbole, because we're prepared to accept that football players can get paid five hundred grand a week. I hate the glorification of some of it. I don't like that we're running around, chucking around figures as if they're just confetti. I think it's a little bit unedifying and a little bit unpalatable, a little bit vulgar, but it's also showbusiness.

People watch it. They're intrigued by it. You know, I can only hear the same rumour once and then I've lost interest in it. It either comes to fruition or it doesn't. So it's remarkable that people keep coming back and watching the same thing. But that's what football is now, that is what it is and is it better or worse for it? I don't know.

You know, the next generation of viewers will tell us. I get the reasons why people are so interested in it because we do live in a slightly vacuous, unsubstantial world where perception is 90 per cent of reality.

Chapter 13

This Contract is Unique But I Am a Unique Player

The Churchill Hotel is a smart hotel in the centre of London. It is popular with wealthy tourists because it is just a short walk to Oxford Street. The most expensive rooms cost £5,000 a night, and in the summer of 2023 the hotel was busier than usual. If you knew who you were looking for you could find a group of men from Saudi Arabia deep in conversation in the hotel's bars and restaurants.

The men weren't your average tourists, and they weren't in London to shop for designer handbags for their wives. They were there to buy something much more precious and difficult to find. They had a budget of £1 billion, and they were in London to buy some of the best footballers in the world. The Churchill Hotel is just across the road from the former headquarters of the Premier League. The owners and directors of its twenty clubs would gather at the hotel regularly for their monthly meetings. In the summer of 2023, there was a new league in town.

Some fans may not have noticed in June when Saudi Arabia's sovereign wealth fund, PIF (the Public Investment

Fund), announced it was effectively taking over four of the country's leading clubs. Within a matter of days Saudi Pro League (SPL) clubs embarked on a shopping spree that threatened to change the face of world football.

I wouldn't call myself an expert on Saudi football, but I did cover one of their national teams way back in 1989. The FIFA U–16 World Championship was being held in Glasgow, and I was one of the TV reporters covering it. I will never forget watching a sixteen-year-old winger called Figo playing for Portugal. The legendary Pelé was in town as an ambassador for the tournament.

The big story for me though was Scotland getting all the way to the final where they were favourites to beat Saudi Arabia. Now the tournament was supposed to be for players sixteen and under, and I was not the only person out of the fifty-eight thousand who were at Hampden Park on Saturday 24 June 1989 who suspected that there had been a mix-up and the Saudis had thought it was for players under twenty-six. There was more facial hair in the Saudi dressing room than on the floor of your local Turkish barber.

Of course, I'm joking. Looking back now, I'm sure everything was above board and fair. It's just that maybe – even after thirty-four years – I still haven't got over the fact that, against all odds, it was the Saudis who ended up lifting the trophy. To say they had to do it the hard way would be an understatement. They came out on top despite going 2–0 down after twenty-five minutes and having a man sent off in the second half. I still remember the drama of the sudden death penalty shoot-out which the Saudis won 5–4 after two sixteen-year-olds, Paul Dickov and Brian O'Neil, missed spot kicks for Scotland.

I have to admit I didn't really think much about Saudi Arabia and their sporting ambitions until 2021 when PIF controversially bought an 80 per cent stake in Newcastle United for £244 million. The level of interest and passion for the game there really hit me when I was in Qatar for the World Cup in the winter of 2022. Saudi Arabia had more fans than any other country at that tournament. More than seventy thousand had made the short journey across the border and the scenes on the streets of Doha were incredible when they beat the eventual winners Argentina – and Lionel Messi – 2–1 in their opening group game.

There were Saudis wherever you went in Doha and all they wanted to talk about was football. If you spent any time with them, it became very clear very quickly that they loved the game with the same passion and intensity as fans from anywhere else in the world. Sometimes in Western Europe we forget that football really is a global game. The Saudis I met were obsessed with the Premier League and English clubs as well as their own teams and national side. The men who run Saudi Arabia had already decided to invest massively in sport before the World Cup in Qatar, but maybe the success of that tournament convinced them to be even bolder and more ambitious with their long-term plans.

Six weeks after Saudi Arabia beat Argentina, Cristiano Ronaldo was sitting in a press conference in Riyadh in a grey suit and a blue silk tie announcing to the world that he had signed to play for Al-Nassr. 'This contract is unique, but I am a unique player,' he said. 'This is a new challenge.'

At thirty-seven, Ronaldo's best days were behind him, but he was still a global superstar and his move to Saudi Arabia made headlines across the world. As one of the two best players in the world for most of his career, Ronaldo had been used to being rewarded handsomely for his extra-ordinary talent but the money on offer at Al-Nassr was truly mind-boggling. Ronaldo signed a two-and-a-half-year contract which could earn him up to £177 million a year. That explosive TV interview he gave which ended his Manchester United career in November 2022 had really paid dividends.

I have to be honest and admit that, like a lot of people, I thought Ronaldo's move was going to be a one-off. I did not anticipate that he was going to start a gold-rush which would see so many players following in his footsteps in the summer of 2023. Publishing deadlines meant Kaveh and I had to finish writing this book at the end of July 2023, when there was still more than a month to go of the summer window. At the time of writing, Riyad Mahrez, Allan Saint-Maximin, Fabinho, Sadio Mané and Neymar are the latest players to move to the SPL.

Mahrez swapped Manchester City for Al-Ahli in a £30 million deal which earned him a tax-free £500,000-a-week four-year contract. That is an incredible amount of money for a thirty-two-year-old player who is approaching the final few years of his playing career. The numbers involved in these deals are almost impossible to get your head round. And when you take a step back and look at the big picture you are left with the impression that some very rich people have hit the jackpot and won the lottery while the rest of the United Kingdom struggles through a cost of living crisis.

What makes what has been happening in Saudi Arabia unprecedented is the fact that there has been an element of central control over the signing of players. In the middle of July 2023, it was announced that Michael Emenalo had been appointed the first SPL director of football. Emenalo had been the technical director at Chelsea and the sporting director at Monaco but in Saudi Arabia he wouldn't be responsible for just one club, he would be the director of football for the whole league.

All SPL clubs are financially backed by the Saudi state and each one was told before the window how much money they would have to spend on players. Club technical staff discussed their needs with the SPL and Emenalo, and transfer targets were shortlisted for the summer. One of Emenalo's jobs is to map and analyse squads and advise clubs on the market value of their targets and the size and length of contracts players should be offered.

Once an offer for a player has been prepared, it has to be centrally approved by the SPL before a deal can be completed. Each club knows its own budget but not that of its rivals. Clubs are discouraged from trying to sign the same players and bid against each other. The majority of money SPL clubs have been spending on players has come from the Ministry of Sport and PIF, but the long-term ambition is for the league to become self-sustainable as it grows through revenue from commercial and sponsorship deals as well as broadcasting contracts. To give you some idea of the huge investment involved so far, PIF announced in October 2022 that it had signed sponsorship agreements with Saudi clubs worth £1.8 billion.

One of the most controversial moves of the summer was Liverpool captain Jordan Henderson moving to Al-Ettifaq at the end of July. Henderson had been an ally for the LGBTQA+ community and had stood up for their rights, yet here he was moving to a country where homosexuality is banned. The Saudis say they are investing in sport because they want to diversify their economy and encourage their population to get more involved in active pursuits. Critics say they are doing it to sportswash their image on the world stage and project soft power to grow their global influence.

Amnesty International has accused Saudi Arabia of embarking on a programme of 'sportswashing to try to obscure its extremely poor human rights record'. A United Nations investigation into the 2018 murder of journalist Jamal Khashoggi said his death 'constituted an extrajudicial killing for which the state of the Kingdom of Saudi Arabia is responsible'.

I am not sure how much research players do before they decide to move to Saudi Arabia, but I would assume that someone like Henderson would have thought long and hard about whether it was the right move for him and his family. Without wishing to be too cynical, I believe almost every player, just like almost every human being, has his price. I have spoken to many former players about the rights and wrongs of playing in Saudi Arabia, and I have yet to meet one who says that they would turn down the kind of money that is being offered to players now.

Henderson will have his reasons for making the decision he has made and I wish him all the best at his new club. I am not going to sit here and judge anyone. I am sure he will want to talk about his reasons for moving to Al-Ettifaq; and maybe one day he will want to speak directly to the people who feel he has let them down. Most footballers I know are interested in just doing their jobs to the best of their abilities and looking after their families. Footballers are human beings just like the rest of us. Some of them care about social causes and politics, and some of them just want to be left alone to get on with their jobs and lives.

The players who have moved to Saudi Arabia will be taking a big step down in class as far as the quality of the football is concerned, but they have been told that the country has big ambitions. Saudi Arabia wants to establish itself as the home of one of the best top ten leagues in the world as quickly as possible. I have spoken to some of the people involved in what is happening in Saudi, and they say that the top of their football pyramid was the last part of their football infrastructure that needed fixing. They are very proud of the fact that their national team beat Argentina at the

World Cup, and they say they are just as proud of the investments which have been made in youth teams, coaching and infrastructure. It is not clear whether Saudi Arabia will bid to host the 2030 World Cup but the ambition to stage the greatest show on earth as soon as possible is certainly there.

While what is happening in Saudi Arabia is a big deal and headline news, I still think we should keep things in perspective. The SPL is not going to challenge the Premier League, the most popular league in the world, any time soon. Halfway through the 2023 summer window, SPL clubs had spent about £200 million on players but that figure was dwarfed by the £1.1 billion that had been spent by the twenty Premier League clubs. Serie A, the Bundesliga, La Liga and Ligue 1 had all spent more money than the eighteen SPL clubs as well.

What sets the SPL apart is the wages on offer to players, especially those in their thirties and, of course, the fact that there is no income tax in Saudi makes it an even more attractive destination. Not every player says yes though when a Saudi club comes calling and the most high-profile examples of that have been Lionel Messi and Kylian Mbappé. French newspaper *L'Equipe* reported in June 2023 that Messi had turned down an incredible €1 billion two-year offer from Al-Hilal to sign for Inter Miami after his Paris Saint-Germain contract ran out.

Kylian Mbappé was offered almost as much to move to the same club, but he said no to Al-Hilal as well. On Saturday 22 July 2023 Al-Hilal decided to try and take advantage of a contract stand-off between PSG and Mbappé by making a world-record €300 million offer for the France captain. Mbappé had been dropped from the club's preseason tour of Japan and South Korea a day earlier because he was refusing to sign a contract extension. PSG were convinced that Mbappé was going to move to Real Madrid on a free transfer in the summer of 2024, and they desperately wanted him to trigger the one-year extension option in his contract to the summer of 2025 so that they could at least get a fee for him when he left. Mbappé was under no legal obligation to extend the contract and PSG responded to his refusal by trying to sell him to whoever wanted him in the summer of 2023. The only problem was that Mbappé didn't have to go anywhere. He could simply hold his nerve, turn down all potential moves and dig his heels in even if PSG threatened that he wouldn't play for them for the whole of the 2023/24 season. Mbappé had set his heart on a move to Real Madrid – again – and not even the prospect earning hundreds of millions of Euros tax free in Riyadh was going to tempt him to change his mind.

Mbappé made it known that he was not interested in meeting representatives from Al Hilal who had come to Paris to discuss a move, even after PSG had given the SPL club permission to speak to the player. Al Hilal's world-record offer was subject to the agreement of a payment schedule between the clubs. It was also conditional on the signing of a contract between the clubs, and the signing of an employment contract between Mbappé and Al Hilal.

Without any talks, let alone an agreement between the player and the Saudi club, the most expensive deal in the history of football never got further than an official offer letter sent electronically from Riyadh to Paris.

Who knows where Saudi Arabia's oil-backed move into football will end? I wouldn't rule them out of trying to invest in the Premier League one day. For the time being, their ambitions seem to be limited to growing the game in their own country as quickly as possible and PIF backing Newcastle United. What the Saudis are doing feels very different to what happened with the Chinese Super League in 2016. There was a gold-rush then too, but it was nothing like this one and quickly ran out of steam. The Chinese government went from encouraging clubs to spend big on foreign players to changing its mind. A combination of new rules, a property market crash and Covid-19 stopped the expansion project in its tracks.

Could the Saudis try to invest in the Premier League one day? It would be extremely difficult but never say never. We have seen venture capitalists and private equity firms investing in leagues, and PIF have effectively taken over golf after the announcement in June 2023 that the Saudi-backed LIV Golf had agreed a controversial merger with the PGA Tour.

Whatever happens next, I want to be covering this story for as long as possible. However, I don't want to end this book talking about business and money. I want to talk about football.

When Kaveh and I were finishing writing this book in the

summer of 2023, we were both shocked to hear of the death of Trevor Francis. It seemed strange to be talking about Al Hilal making a €300 million bid for Mbappé in the morning and the death of Britain's first £1 million player in the afternoon.

Trevor played for two clubs who are close to our hearts, and we both had the pleasure of watching him play. We were also fortunate enough to meet him after he retired. We both told him what a great player he was and how much we had enjoyed watching him play. Neither of us asked him about his famous £1 million move from Birmingham City to Nottingham Forest in 1979. It didn't even cross our minds to bring it up. I'm sure when you meet your heroes you will be talking about football and not transfers as well.

Fraser Robertson was a great friend and colleague.

He worked with Jim at STV in Glasgow and with
Jim and Kaveh at Sky Sports News in London.
He was a hard-working, conscientious man who loved
his family, his job and playing golf – very good golf.

Fraser died in March 2019 aged 47.

He is very much missed.

This book is dedicated to Fraser.